PRAISE FOR
ZEN AT THE END OF RELIGION

"Trappist monk Thomas Merton wrote, 'Zen is a way of insight.' Then he suggested what Zen is not: a system or method to be institutionalized, the way western society has domesticated religion. James Ford's insightful and honest introduction to this venerable tradition of meditation and inner transformation just might help us see what Merton meant—and why Zen can be a great blessing for our time, even for those who identify as spiritual but not religious." —CARL McCOLMAN, author of *The New Big Book of Christian Mysticism* and *Read the Bible Like a Mystic*

"James Ford has long been an honest and thoughtful voice on matters spiritual and religious. In *Zen at the End of Religion* he shines a light on Zen as a path for those who are alienated from religious institutions but are still seeking—something. Something deep, boundless, intimate. *Zen at the End of Religion* is a clear and authentic introduction to Zen." —BARBARA O'BRIEN, author of *The Circle of the Way: A Concise History of Zen from the Buddha to the Modern World*

"When I hear James Ford's words, something in me wakes up. He has the rare ability to communicate something that is much larger than himself. We are all lucky to be in contact with this gift." —GESSHIN CLAIRE GREENWOOD, author of *Bow First, Ask Questions Later*

"James Ishmael Ford has given us re-introduction—to living and twenty-first century America. In t dite, he plays in the deep waters

delight, born of decades of practice and teaching. This delight is contagious!" —**ZENSHIN FLORENCE CAPLOW**, author of *The Hidden Lamp: Twenty-Five Centuries of Awakened Women*

ZEN
AT THE END OF RELIGION

AN INTRODUCTION FOR THE CURIOUS,
THE SKEPTICAL, AND THE SPIRITUAL
BUT NOT RELIGIOUS

JAMES ISHMAEL FORD

MONKFISH
BOOK PUBLISHING COMPANY
RHINEBECK, NEW YORK

Zen at the End of Religion: An Introduction for the Curious, the Skeptical, and the Spiritual but Not Religious Copyright © 2025 by James Ishmael Ford

All rights reserved. No part of this book may be used or reproduced in any manner without the consent of the publisher except for in critical articles or reviews. Contact the publisher for information.

Paperback ISBN 9781958972762
eBook ISBN 9781958972779

Library of Congress Cataloging-in-Publication Data

Names: Ford, James Ishmael, author.
Title: Zen at the end of religion : an introduction for the curious, the skeptical, and the spiritual but not religious / James Ishmael Ford.
Description: Rhinebeck, New York : Monkfish Book Publishing Company, [2025]
Identifiers: LCCN 2025000509 (print) | LCCN 2025000510 (ebook) | ISBN 9781958972762 (paperback) | ISBN 9781958972779 (ebook)
Subjects: LCSH: Zen Buddhism--United States. | Religion--United States.
Classification: LCC BQ9261.U6 F67 2025 (print) | LCC BQ9261.U6 (ebook) | DDC 294.3/9270973--dc23/eng/20250123
LC record available at https://lccn.loc.gov/2025000509
LC ebook record available at https://lccn.loc.gov/2025000510

Book and cover design by Colin Rolfe

Monkfish Book Publishing Company
22 East Market Street, Suite 304
Rhinebeck, New York 12572
(845) 876-4861
monkfishpublishing.com

For
Robert Baker Aitken
Dairyū Chōtan Gyōun Roshi

CONTENTS

PART ONE:
THE COLLAPSE OF RELIGIONS

Waking Up	3
The Religious and the Spiritual	5
Toward a Naturalistic Perennialism	10
Why Zen?	15
The Varieties of Zen	20

PART TWO:
THE SECRET TEACHINGS OF THE ZEN WAY

The Heart of the Buddhist Way	27
Four Noble Truths	30
Five Hundred Lives	34
Ten Ox Herding Pictures	42
An Empty World	46
So, Is Zen a Religion?	50

PART THREE:
THE WAYS OF ZEN

Zen's Mystic Heart	57
Sit Down and Become Buddha	60
A Note on the Use of Chairs	65
Taking a Walk on the Wild Side	69
Breathing Zen	73
Samadhi	78

Koan and Huatou	86
Great Doubt, Faith, and Energy	92
Ritual and Liturgy	97
Lovingkindness	102
Communities of Practice	109
Retreats and a Note on What to Do When You Can't	117
Waking Up in the Kitchen	122
Spiritual Directors and Teachers	127
The Matter of Waking Up and Growing Up	134

PART FOUR: DIRECT POINTING

A Koan about Toilet Paper	143
A Koan about What Is Alive	147
A Koan about Zen Teachers	153
A Koan about a Stone Crypt	158
A Koan about a Bunch of Bodhisattvas Taking a Bath	165

PART FIVE:
FINDING OUR WAY AT THE END OF RELIGION

Zen as Magical Realism	171
Zen in a New World	175
Conclusion: The Ox's Tail	181
Acknowledgements	187

PART ONE
THE COLLAPSE OF RELIGIONS

We're in a liminal moment, when the grip of our old religions has loosened. In this moment we're able to see things a bit more clearly, and maybe even to sort wheat and chaff. Here we can explore some important questions, perhaps critical questions for lives that matter. Among them: What is religion? What is spirituality?

And most of all. Why this life?

Why?

WAKING UP

When the fully enlightened ones do not appear,
And when the disciples have disappeared,
The wisdom of the self-enlightened ones
Will arise completely without a teacher.
(Nagarjuna)[1]

A hundred thousand years ago, perhaps two hundred thousand. Maybe it was a million. Possibly even longer ago. No one remembers precisely. Although we know it was in Africa. Probably near the Great Rift.

A human being woke up. We don't know her name. But she is our common ancestor. We all live within her lineage.

In my dreaming she looked up from her work, perhaps she was tending a child. Maybe she was cooking a meal. It was something to do with the busy of our lives. She paused. And she looked up from her work. And at that moment the morning star kissed the moon. And the world changed.

Everything was the same. And yet it changed. Everything was the same, and yet, now it was all new. She saw we were all of us, humans and plants and animals and the dirt under our feet and the stars above us, intimate. More intimate than words can convey. Although the poets can come close.

The major projects of those aspects of cultures we call religions are mostly about cultural cohesion, definition, and boundaries.

---
[1] Nagarjuna, *The Fundamental Wisdom of the Middle Way, Nagarjuna's Mulamadhyamakakarika*, trans. and commentary by Jay L. Garfield (Oxford University Press, 1995), 56.

But at the same time there has always been that aspect of religion concerned with the deep. Call it mystical. Call it the spiritual within religions. It is as natural as natural can be, common, perennial, intimate human encounter.

It is our ancient human awakening into intimacy.

It's always something deeply personal. Personal while always inescapably part of the web of relationships. Not exactly one. Not precisely two. But, really, it's not that complicated, it's all about intimacy.

Intimacy.

THE RELIGIOUS AND THE SPIRITUAL

> *"Are you old?"*
> *"I guess I am."*
> *"Are you going to die?"*
> *"I guess I am, but not yet."*
> *"Don't worry, you'll do it really good."*
> (Book of Householder Koans)[1]

I have a friend, a Unitarian minister. When on an airplane or other situation in close company with strangers, he is sometimes asked what he does. As in what he does for a living. He invariably replies that he's a garbage man. It doesn't always stop the conversation. But it certainly slows it down.

Fewer than a third of Americans have a high opinion of clergy. Priests, ministers, rabbis, imams; they pretty much only rank above politicians, lawyers, and journalists. Clergy and the religious institutions they serve are not thought well of in our moment. Today, churches in Europe are largely empty. And they are rapidly emptying in North America.

And not just there and here. A recent headline in *The Japan Times* screams, "Is Religion in Japan in Irreversible Decline?" It seems Japanese Buddhist temples are emptying out there at about the same rate as Christian churches are declining in North America and Europe.

Religion, certainly organized religions, are in turmoil. The

---

[1] Eve Myonen Marko, Wendy Egyoku Nakao, *Book of Householder Koans* (Monkfish, 2020), 182.

whole idea of institutional religions is being challenged. At least in some parts of the world. Certainly, in most of the global north. Over the coming decades of the twenty-first century much of what in America has been called "mainline Protestantism" will at the very least be radically reduced. Many religious institutions hang by a thread. Some venerable denominations may fully disappear this century.

Today, the fastest growing demographic in the United States is "None," as in "none of the above." For some Nones the whole idea of religions is nothing but bad news. And the sooner we all outgrow them, the better. For some, too much lingering hurt from too much abuse to give religions any time. For some, they've just drifted away from the religions they grew up in. There's no great energy one way or another. Religious claims on the imagination and heart are loosening, and often have been lost entirely.

Religion is a many-splendored term, so a precise definition is elusive. For many it is the most obvious example of what's wrong in our culture, how people are controlled. For others it's that powerful thing which hurts but is otherwise irrelevant. And there is much more to what religion has been and is and might yet be. I believe a functional definition is that religion is traditionally that part of a culture concerned with meaning and purpose.

In cultures identified with one religion in particular the task of religion is to establish one's place in that culture through various rites of recognition. There are at least vestiges of this sense in all modern major religions. Defining who is in and who is out is where much of the hurt that people experience happens. This is also where people increasingly see irrelevance.

At the same time, among the Nones there are a lot of people who sense there is within religions, or maybe simply aligned with religions, something that speaks to deep matters within our human hearts. It is that sense of meaning and purpose which is the original work of religion. This sense is mainly captured today in the phrase "spiritual but not religious." Spirituality is where people find the Why of their, of our, lives. The big why, with that capital "W."

Spiritual is, of course, a slippery term as well. Perhaps even more vague than religion, which we can at least identify by its institutions. Spirituality and spirit seem flighty, skittish, ready in a moment to disappear in a flutter of wings. That why, that capital "w" Why can be ephemeral. And at the same time, it can be the most important thing in our lives.

Reasonably, perhaps. Etymologically, spiritual means breath. And spirituality is concerned with those parts of religions that seem to enliven us. Spiritual is evocative, but also elusive. It is fair to say spirituality is about those aspects of our lives that bring meaning and depth to who we are and how we live.

As I dig deeper into spiritual but not religious, I see three different groupings for whom the term fits. No doubt there are further nuances, but these seem particularly to the point. They are all united in suspicion of religious institutions, whether church or temple or mosque. But each has differing ways of engaging what that enlivening, that spiritual might mean.

The first group is deeply suspicious of religious institutions. But they are interested in various spiritual claims, especially what coalesced in the later twentieth century as New Age. This includes interest in alternative states of consciousness, and alternative approaches to spirituality, often including a focus on alternative approaches to health. They also tend to be wildly eclectic.

The second group brings that suspicion of religious institutions, as well. But they are drawn to the world's mystical traditions. Their pursuit mostly focuses on reading, sometimes quite widely. They see wisdom that appears to have some commonalities in Buddhism, early Taoist literature, the Advaita forms of Hinduism, among Muslim Sufis, within Medieval Hasidic Judaism and the Kabbalists, as well as in the writings of fourth and fifth century Christian desert fathers and mothers, and many mystical writers following. To begin a long list.

In this broad ranging mystical interest, they also are eclectic. This group is frequently, maybe usually concerned with finding spirituality as an underlying unity in religions, so their eclecticism often becomes syncretistic.

Some of these touch that matter of our ancient ancestor. The one who looked up and saw the moon and the morning star kissing.

Who woke up.

And resolved the burning question of Why.

The third group also bring that suspicion of religious institutions. This suspicion of institutions is the negative through line of the spiritual but not religious. But here it also comes with the positive sense there are currents in the old religions, currents that can open hearts and minds in powerful and transformative ways. They read the same books as the second group. And they have intimations there may be some kind of perennial truth to be found.

What distinguishes them from the second group is that they often feel driven to know what those mystics speak of for themselves. They want to understand that Why. They want to drink from the ancient well and know for themselves whether the waters are cool or warm.

They not only study religions and their various spiritual perspectives, but they seek spiritual disciplines, practices like prayer and meditation. They also share that intimation of some kind of deep unity, a sense that we're all taking different paths, but that maybe we're ascending the same mountain. Some of these might joke with their interests in spiritual disciplines that they're religious but not spiritual. And in all this they share that eclectic and often syncretistic sense.

Now each of these groupings overlap to one degree or

another. And especially within the second and third groups are people who cherish the gifts brought to us by modern science. It can even be part of what shook them loose from their native religions. If they see any kind of perennial wisdom, mainly they intuit it is probably some form of a naturalistic perennialism. The perennial here is understood as some heart wisdom common to our humanity. But often as some natural thing where probably no specific tradition could get it entirely right. It is both a critical approach and an approach that can be humble, and deeply curious.

There are many, and I count myself among these, who intuit some deep spiritual calling. But at the same time see it all occurring within a broad and generously understood natural world. Human religious institutions are where the teachings tend to reside. This even seems important. Institutions are the repositories of the stories, the traditions, and the disciplines. And they are subject to all the same limitations of any other natural thing. Religious institutions are all flawed. And too often the needs of the institution obscure, or even perversely, hide that spiritual insight.

With that here we are.

TOWARD A NATURALISTIC PERENNIALISM

> *In studying the Perennial Philosophy we can begin either at the bottom, with practice and morality; or at the top, with a consideration of metaphysical truths; or, finally, in the middle, at the focal point where mind and matter, action and thought have their meeting place in human psychology.*
> (Aldous Huxley)[1]

That story about our first ancestor? The details come from the dream time. But awakening, that is our common inheritance as human beings. It comes to us in dreams. It comes to us in the waking night. It comes to us in the moment. This moment. It is the great gift.

What it means has been reflected on for lifetimes. The most important thing has been our own understanding. But a second question has been, how does this happen? How do we best understand it? Out of this we have told ourselves stories. These stories become the foundation points of many religions. Or at least it seems like that.

People have approached the matter in many different ways. In the West, Plato and Aristotle both wrestled with the questions of a possible perennial wisdom. As have many since. In the fifteenth century, Marsilio Ficino argued there was an underlying

---

[1] Aldous Huxley, *The Perennial Philosophy* (Chatto and Windus, 1946), 7.

unity to the world's religions. One of his students coined a term for this, the *philosophia perennis*, the perennial philosophy. People have argued for some kind of Perennialism ever since.

An influential subset of Perennialism is Traditionalism. Traditionalism is a word with many definitions. It usually speaks to some form of conservativism. It sometimes is associated with right wing political perspectives, and probably always is marked with a privileging of revelation over reason. In considering some common current to our spiritual lives, it's worth looking at least briefly at both Perennialism and Traditionalism.

My first brush with Traditionalism arose when I read Huston Smith's magnum opus, the *Religions of Man*, still in print as *The World's Religions*. This book was first published in 1958 and has stood several tests of time to remain the most likely book an English-speaking reader will turn to in order to learn about the world's great faiths.

A perennialist current runs through Smith's book. On the one hand, I think it points in the right direction, at least broadly speaking, when it suggests there are common truths that each religion touch. I find it hard to ignore those commonalities, especially when approaching the deeper matters of our heart's longing. And Smith does this with sympathy and a broad knowledge of the religions he addresses.

This perennial insight is a big reason I would eventually find myself a Unitarian Universalist as well as a Zen Buddhist. Unitarian Universalism is the great magpie spiritual tradition, open to the possibility of many truths, and of the possibility of a common truth. On the other hand, as someone who has actually engaged in some depth several of the world's major spiritualities, it seems pretty obvious to me that there is not in fact a single mountain. We're all following separate paths up to its summit.

There are lots of different mountains.

And with that I've come to some other hard conclusions.

Some spiritual paths and their disciplines are more useful than others. Which is why Zen Buddhism and its particular disciplines remains the core of my actual interior life. In my life, Zen has proven most useful for digging into the heart matter. I also love that magpie quality of Unitarian Universalism. But I've found I also need a tap root in order to grow deep. For me that has been a spare Zen Buddhism, with equal attention to the Zen Buddhism and the "spare."

Trying to understand this common thread is complicated, filled with wrong turns and dead ends. For me the best example of the problems with Perennialism is Huston Smith's *The World's Religions*. As I noted, for many years those of us interested in the world's religions had our first glimpses into the richness offered by the world spiritualities. For good reason it has continued in print for years and has altogether sold over two million copies. It was a great help to me. I cannot say how grateful I am for Professor Smith's book.

And. What he doesn't reveal in the book is that he is a Traditionalist, a form of Perennialism that, frankly, while I find very attractive in some ways, also has some serious problems. They bring out all the problems with the perennialist impulse.

Chief among those problems comes from trying to crowbar all the world's religions together into one lovely jewel of many facets. This is not so. There is no coherent singular message. And so, his book, which is admirable in so many ways, and, again, for which I remain endlessly grateful, when it comes to Buddhism struggles to force it into Smith's perennialism.

Professor Smith believed, I'm quite sure, right down to the soles of his feet that there is a true religion under all religions. I can even go with that, up to a point. But for him that universal thing is a mystical theism. And what he doesn't say as a Traditionalist is that this theism comes to us through revelation. Because of that the chapter on Buddhism is deeply marred by his, it feels, desperate reach for theistic elements in Buddhism. Which exist, but which cannot by any stretch be considered normative.

At this point in my life the issue is this: I do believe a form of religious perennialism, it is what I see as the spiritual within religion, and what I'm calling a naturalistic perennialism. I believe there are currents of religion that are rooted in our biology. And as something natural, it is something that people can find within all religions. And actually I find it the heart birthing of all religions. While I hope it would therefore be obvious, this deep current should be available without any religion at all. It comes with our birthing into the human world.

There are a number of these universal currents, some go toward ethics—what I see as an innate sense of the "fair," a sense that things should be harmonious, that what is good for the goose is good for the gander kind of proto-morality. This is confusingly coupled with a deeply held desire to get one up on others, and with that an inclination to cheat. I believe pretty much all religious ethics arise out of these two things existing in tension.

Rather more important is what is at the heart of the mystical, and by mystical, I mean quite narrowly an apprehension of a root to all our individual consciousnesses. For most of the world's religions this root is seen as God, and as profoundly personal. Hence Professor Smith's theistic perennialism and more specifically his traditionalism and its esoteric wisdoms.

Buddhism shows this intimate encounter does not have to be experienced that way. And, for me, points again to our biology. We seem to have within the structures of our brains an ability to see at the same time that we are different and distinct and acting in our own interests, that there is a common place we exist within, an intimacy so profound it is fair, if perhaps ultimately misleading, to call it one.

As to Traditionalism, while I don't believe at all in some single current of truth revealed over the ages, Traditionalism nonetheless offers some very important perspectives. Perspectives I believe need to be considered by anyone following the intimate way. Especially for anyone confronted, as we are, with a wealth of spiritual options. Where so many are contradictory, either internally or on the face of it with other traditions. And all cutting several ways.

Here is where I find important guidance in Traditionalism. They assert one needs to align with a specific religion, and they believe one needs to seek initiation into that tradition. And then to live within it. I find wisdom here. There seems to be a deep truth that the universal is pretty much only met within a particular. Where the Traditionalists go wrong, in my estimation, is their radical rejection of modernity and reason. This later part has led them down some very dark alleys.

Again, I find the first part speaks to some genuine truths about us.

I suspect it starts with the fact that the universal is only ever encountered within the specific. There is no enlightenment. There is only personal encounter with openness. And beyond that we are constantly in danger of following our own appetites. By consciously binding ourselves to a tradition, we are instead constantly challenged about our own views about any given thing.

Magic happens when we take the tradition seriously. I see awakening happening without any particular tradition being at the heart of it. And awakening itself does just happen. Still, living into it, growing deeper, making a life with our discovery of our intimate boundlessness, usually calls for an alignment with a tradition. And this is where Zen enters the picture.

WHY ZEN?

How strange, how strange!
The sermon of the non-sentient is miraculous.
If we try to hear it with ears, it is impossible
    to hear;
But when we hear it with eyes, all things
    find their place.
(Keizan Jokin)[1]

There's a social media meme that makes the rounds every once in a while. There are a couple of versions. The one I most like has two images. In the first there are three people in a car. The one at the driver's wheel is a man in a suit, looking annoyed. He's labeled "Theravada." Which is a type of Buddhism.

Next to him is a woman nicely dressed. She's labeled "Mahayana," another type of Buddhism. She's trying to push away the third figure, leaning over from the back seat. He's wearing glittery glasses and a giant feather boa. Feather boa person is labeled "Vajrayana," which is basically the Buddhism of Tibet and Mongolia.

The second picture shows James Dean leaning on his motorcycle, with a cigarette hanging from his lip. He's labeled "Zen." When I hear the word Zen used in conversation, the word is usually meant to mean cool. For many Zen is the essence of the spiritual but not religious.

Zen is in fact a lot of things. But most of all it is about that

---

[1] The Transmission of the Lamp, Case 38, author's version.

noticing and waking. It is an expression of the intimate way. Zen is a form of Buddhism that arose in China and has traveled to Japan, Korea, and Vietnam. And then from there has come West.

In the East, Zen's institutions meet the problems of modernity. In China all religions are controlled by the state. Or, at least, the state tries. In Korea, Buddhism, including Zen, is being given a serious run for its money by fundamentalist forms of Protestant Christianity. And at the same time, as an emerging part of the global north, all religions in Korea are showing fracture lines and the beginnings of their own Nones. In Japan, as a full-on part of the global north, we get those headlines about decline of religions, including Zen Buddhism.

And Zen is also taking new shapes. That dangling cigarette Zen is just one. I believe this kaleidoscopic range of possibility is the gift found in that collapsing of religious institutions. Or, if not collapsing, certainly shaken to the foundations. A lot is happening. People are looking across schools. Forms that have developed in one cultural context are finding new life among other people.

It is possible here in the West to practice Zen in very similar ways to how it's been done in China or Korea or Vietnam or Japan for a very long time. It's possible to find communities with lineage connections to Asia but are wildly experimental. Increasingly this is most common. There are hybrid practices. And all of these are in varying degree in conversation with each other and the larger spiritual world.

I believe what Zen offers is among the most compelling range of adaptations arising in this uncertain moment. Zen in its several forms is still rooted into the mists of history, often deeply. But also in this vulnerable moment, Zen is open to new expressions. Sometimes these can be very compelling for some among the spiritual but not religious.

Zen offers something to those who have seen the failures of

the old religions, but who intuit some profound spiritual core within those religions. Zen brings ancient teachings that can be seen as a dynamic living spiritual current. Perhaps one of the clearest expressions of that naturalist perennialism. This all turns on how we understand ourselves and the world. Much of this turns on what in Zen is called Buddha nature. That is, what are we really?

I understand when the Japanese first encountered Europeans in the sixteenth century there was a debate as to whether Europeans had Buddha nature. Europeans had their own questions about whether non-Europeans had souls. We humans kind of do that.

Within Buddhism there was for a long time a question about what wakes up. Some drew a line between sentience and non-sentience. The first thought was that something had to have consciousness in order to awaken. Of course it was not then and is still in no settled way clear just what the mystery of consciousness really is. That led to a long debate over where the line might be. It has proven to be very hard.

With that another question arose. Isn't everything connected? Aren't we all in this together? We, us, the humans. But also, animals. And plants. And of course, the very ground on which we walk. The sun, the stars, and the moon. Aren't they all part of the great matter?

The Mahayana resolved this by excluding nothing. Which, does, after all, follow the logic all the way. We're all caught up in the buzz of causes and conditions and consequences, everything is caught up in the buzz. We humans may be unique in having a problem with that ultimate disequilibrium of rising and falling, creating, and dying. But we're all in the mess together.

And with that the use of words began to shift. In Keizan's poem about the sermon of the non-sentient, we hear an echo of another face of the truths of existence. When we speak of non-sentience in Zen, we're often pointing to the place of the great boundless, of emptiness.

That thing which unites us all. Within. Around. Touching. Interpenetrating.

Which brings me to the original thesis of this book. Religions are falling apart. We are in a moment where the mechanisms and institutions of our spiritual lives are laid bare. At least some of them. A tide has gone out, and we're seeing what's around us. One thing that becomes apparent if we're paying attention, is how religion is a cultural phenomenon. And, yes, many intuit that there is something important that mostly arises within religions, or at least in their vicinity. What we call "spiritual." Spiritual for all practical matters, is a human thing.

This also raises questions of relativity. If all things are in one sense equal, are they not also equally meaningless? What about the dust mote, the AIDS virus, a black hole, and you or me? It seems much of what has been reflected on here, maybe all of it, is from an anthropocentric perspective. We don't have the earth at the center, we don't have the sun, we have us.

It really seems that within the dynamic of the universe every point within existence is the actual center of the universe. I don't pretend to understand the physics. But as an aspect of our lived human psychology, I very much get it.

It is very hard for us to separate ourselves from the center of things. But one of the gifts of our moment, where everything feels to be falling apart, is that we do see a little behind the curtain. This wondrous ability to observe ourselves opens us to the mysterious currents we call spiritual. This allows us to consider possibilities not currently featured in our culture. Our cultures.

But there is another haunting truth. No one is the star of this show. We might be the center of the universe, but so is everyone and everything else. While nothing works quite like denial—for a while. At some point we find it wise being full-on present to what is.

We know we are subject to sickness and old age and death. We know we are on a small rock spinning around a middling star, itself circling some massive black hole. And, who knows? There are other motions, which might be other circlings.

And. Very quickly our little Newtonian universe begins to fall apart in the face of very strange things. Rising and falling, but even here, in strange ways.

Sickness, old age, death, and awakening. Meaning and meaninglessness are human constructs. Ways we meet the world. Not the world itself. The world of which we are a part.

So, what about when Zen, no matter what kind of Zen, every version of it falls apart? When it's forgotten? It is, after all, found within human cultural constructs. Which change. So. Maybe not in our lifetime, but eventually.

It doesn't seem hard to see a day when the word Zen is forgotten. At least for us to have an idea of that day. Vanished, along with other words we think pretty important at this moment. It all passes. Given enough time we humans will be no more. There will be a time when our little planet itself is consumed by our dying and expanding star.

So?

I find as I turn to what is, as I let go of the speculative part of this, and simply allow my being to be present, many feelings and thoughts race across my brain, electric currents flashing and sparking.

How strange, how strange! A miracle. Sung out of dying stars and the falling rain.

Just this is always just this. Even after the words have burned away. The possible spiritual within religions.

THE VARIETIES OF ZEN

*London Bridge is falling down,
Falling down, falling down,
London Bridge is falling down,
My fair lady.*
(Traditional English nursery rhyme)

Zen has evolved in the West in some interesting ways. I'm fascinated how the traditional schools of Zen mostly have found at least a toehold. Some are aggressively presenting varying adaptations of their schools for western hearers. Japanese Soto and Korean Taego immediately leap to mind. What will come of these missions is yet to be written.

There are other Zen schools that clearly belong to the Mahayana, but are more culturally hybrid. There is that interesting rise of householder Zen. Something I particularly find interesting. Even exciting.

Then there is the rise of non-Buddhist practitioners. I've met Muslims who are devoted Zen practitioners without ever not being Muslim. I've known Hindu Zen practitioners. The combinations of spiritualities that find alignment with Zen's gifts appears endless.

But there are three principal groupings of such people. There is a deep secular interest in Zen stripped of its religiosity. This is often aligned with a concern for and investigation of how Zen's approach to the mind and western views of psychology encounter each other. And among religions both Jews and Christians have found aspects of the discipline compelling. And each brings gifts into our moment. It's worth noticing these forms of Zen beyond the bounds we normally think of as Buddhist.

First are secular Zen practitioners.

Secular Zen is a Zen stripped of all "religious" content. Or nearly all. I've found it wise to try and avoid being completely categorical. We humans seem to have a near endless capacity for exceptions to rules. What secular Zen generally means is a conscious rejection of anything that might be perceived as supernatural. But it often includes stripping away any culturally identified elements such as bowing or chanting in ancient languages, or sometimes chanting at all. For good and for ill.

Secular Zen generally approaches the tradition as a psychological phenomenon. Each of these three aspects of non-Buddhist Zen are the product of a dialogue. For secular Zen the dialogue is with western psychology. Among the writers about Zen and psychology there are researchers like James Austin, author of many books starting with *Zen and the Brain*, and the first generation of western-born and trained practitioner teachers like Charlotte Joko Beck and Toni Packer. I'm very fond of Barry Magid, a psychotherapist and successor to Joko Roshi, who offers Zen as a vital discipline within a psychological context.

Zen psychology brings a materialist assumption to the conversation. And with that, secular and psychologized versions of Zen bring challenges to traditional religious language. They push those of us who practice Zen to meet the dichotomies, both perceived and real, between our received traditions and what actually presents in our lives.

What you see is indeed often what you get.

The result can be rich, pushing us toward what might be a nonreducible core of what Zen's famous enlightenment experience is and is not. And sometimes it is simply reductive, creating artificial divides where none naturally occur. Sometimes slipping completely away from the project of awakening to a mild mitigation of anxiety. There's a growing literature out of the meeting of Zen and its assertions and the varieties of western psychological schools. Some seem to be very important.

The other emerging Zen traditions take advantage of that reductive impulse at its best. They reveal within a quest for the bare truths of Zen, and the complexity of our lived lives, how several stories bring us into some uncomfortable proximities. Sometimes with intriguing, and on occasion, wonderful results.

So, Jewish Zen. I sometimes tell people I learned all of my Yiddish when living in a Buddhist monastery. At first they often think I'm telling a small joke. While I enjoy the irony, the fact is it isn't a joke. It's where I learned nearly all the Yiddish terms that are part of my vocabulary, and there's a fair amount of it in my vocabulary. This came along with a deep appreciation of the Jewish tradition especially at the edge where it meets Zen.

With the great boom of Zen in the 1960s many young Jews found themselves drawn to the discipline. Some felt they were converting to Buddhism. Many, however, perhaps most, did not. Even when some ordained as monastics and others in the priestly traditions, many, maybe most felt they remained Jewish. Among the more notable might be the poet and musician Leonard Cohen, and the Zen masters Norman Zoketsu Fischer, Alan Hozan Senauke, and Bernard Tetsugen Glassman.

Zen practitioner and psychotherapist Brenda Shoshanna explains, "A Jewish heart is warm, giving, human, devoted to family and friends and filled with the longing for the well-being of all. A Zen eye is fresh, direct, spontaneous, planted in the present moment. It is unencumbered by ideas, beliefs, tradition, hopes or expectations."[1] She then offers how "These practices are like two wings of a bird, both are needed for it to fly."

Here we find a stripped-down Zen, in a sense similar to that

---

[1] Brenda Shoshanna, *Jewish Dharma: A Guide to the Practice of Judaism and Zen* (Da Capo: 2008), 2.

found in secular forms, rooted in disciplines of presence and implying if not promising a saving encounter in that presence. And it suggests something might be lost with only those two things. Or would be lost, except here it is complemented where there was a lack from the stripping away. Now met and enriched by a generous application of Jewish principles. For instance, it is an invitation into that ancient story of exodus from bondage into freedom mutually found in Zen and Judaism. Something that can totally be seen as Zen. And is totally Jewish. Here Zen is not exactly grafted onto another tradition, but is more brought together in intimate, new, and exciting ways.

Zen Christians become the third emerging hybridized Zen community. For North American readers, the work of the Catholic monk Thomas Merton might come to mind. But he just begins a list that includes people who've moved well beyond appreciation of Zen to become dedicated practitioners, and in an increasing number of cases to become lineage holders, acknowledged as Zen teachers and Zen masters.

The German Jesuit Hugo Enomiya-Lassalle was the first Christian to be acknowledged within lineage as a master on the Zen way. But many have followed. The former Jesuit Rubén Hábito, Redemptorist priest Patrick Hawk, and Our Lady's Missionaries sister Elaine MacInnis begin a significant list. In one case a substantial lineage is emerging from the teaching line of the Jesuit Robert Kennedy.

Close definitions of how Zen and Secular, Jewish, and Christian perspectives meet, merge or do not, are elusive. To know where each of these teachers and practitioners, secular-identified, Jewish, or Christian fit into a larger understanding of Zen, one needs to ask each of them.

What is critical to note is that many of them are counted within traditional Zen lineages as Zen masters. And with that, hints of a Zen that is not exclusively Buddhist. Or, at the very least, there is some part of the Zen way that flows between the differing religions and even secularity.

At the same time the throughline of Zen is Buddhism. But even the Buddhism of Zen finds it has different faces in modernity. There are more traditional forms, often closely tied to the institutions of the countries from which they come. Even in the West. The religious calendars found in monasteries and temples follow those ancient inheritances. Sometimes folding in western holidays. Sometimes not.

And with this such questions as whether rebirth and karma are literal or metaphorical descriptions of inner states are not questions at all. They are part of the gift being transmitted.

But there are growing communities and individuals that are less sure of such things while transmitting the practices and often many of the traditional forms. So, you see festivals like Obon, which involves honoring the ancestors, folded in with Halloween. This introduces new nuances, not dissimilar to when early Indian Buddhist missionaries adapted Chinese spiritual words, like Tao for Dharma. Sometimes the dates move, as well.

We're in a time of a hundred flowers. And it will be a while before anyone can say with certainty where the weeds might be.

PART TWO
THE SECRET TEACHINGS OF THE ZEN WAY

There are currents of insight that appear to rise naturally among human beings. Although the different spiritual traditions explain it all differently. They offer different ways to notice and then grow deep. In this chaotic time where civilizations are shifting and often it feels like the world is coming apart, the traditions of Zen seem especially clear and useful.

THE HEART OF THE BUDDHIST WAY

A non-Buddhist asked the Buddha with all of her heart, "I don't ask about words, I don't ask about the emptiness of words." The Buddha sat quietly. The non-Buddhist responded, "Your kindness is boundless. You have scattered the clouds of my confusion and have opened the way for me." She bowed deeply and left the world honored one's presence. The Buddha's attendant, Ananda, then asked, "Sir, what did she see that caused her to praise you?" The Buddha replied, "She is like the finest horse, that takes off at full gallop, with just the shadow of a whip."
(Gateless Gate)[1]

Zen is about awakening. Always.

It is about the same awakening found by our first ancestor in untold antiquity. And it is what has been found by sages and seers across the globe over the many years. Each, importantly, encounter the mystery in their own place, in their own way. It is a universalist vision. Not owned by any one in particular. Its expression has evolved in specific cultures. And is very much the fruit of those specific cultures.

---

[1] Gateless Gate, Case 32. Also in the *Blue Cliff Record*, as Case 65. Author's version.

Zen's way in to awakening is at heart a Chinese version of Buddhism. China, that ancient civilization rooted in practicality. The original nation of shop keepers. And at the same time a nation of poets. Both are critical to Zen. China's two indigenous religions show that in high profile. Confucianism is always practical, it's all about right relationships with a heavy emphasis on here and now. And Taoism is a counterpoint, all about the dark places, flowing water, and dreaming the mother of the ten thousand things. Shop keepers and poets. A cradle for the Zen way.

It cannot be overstated. Zen is heavily shaped by China, and particularly indigenous Chinese religions. That said, and its importance cannot be overstated, Zen's beating heart is found within the Mahayana schools of Buddhism. Zen forms in China, but its deepest roots are in the Indian foothills of the Himalayas. So, knowing just a little about Buddhism's roots is critical for any understanding of Zen.

Buddhism's founder, Gautama Siddhartha, the Buddha, lived somewhere between three, or four, or maybe five hundred years before the birth of Jesus, near what is now the border between northern India and Nepal. There are no independent accounts of his life. Everything we know is contained in the sacred writings of the tradition. None of them were written down until hundreds of years after he died. And none of the texts we have are in Magadhi Prakrit, the language he spoke.

So, we don't have that much certainty about the Buddha and his life. Although the mainstream of scholars is certain, or close enough to certain, that the Buddha was a real person. He probably was born to wealth and power. Later he renounced it to become a wandering mendicant. He had some great awakening.

Awakening. There are several versions of what that awakening was. The Zen schools tell of an extended period of meditating in the shade of a tree when he looked up at the morning star.

Some shift occurred. With this he exclaimed, "At this moment I and all the beings of this great earth have attained the way!"

There are those other versions of what he said out of this moment. But Zen's great insight is into the heart of a matter that exists right here, where we find a human sitting under a tree and looking at the morning light. Here and in this place as the birthing of great miracles.

The traditions say the Buddha was thirty-five when he had this transformative experience. And he is believed to have lived for eighty years. So, forty-five years of assimilating this understanding and sharing it with others. He gathered around him a group of followers, and constantly taught. He first created a company of monks, and later added in a company of nuns. He moved among the poor and the rich and powerful. His admirers listened and repeated his teachings. Eventually they were written down.

There is a wonderful brief summary of his teachings. They are foundational to any understanding of Zen. Of course, Buddhism and Zen are vastly larger than this. But it carries the core of his message. They describe the heart of awakening as expressed in Zen.

They are called the Four Noble Truths.

FOUR NOBLE TRUTHS

> *"Recognizing the World Wound also turns us away from a sense of exclusiveness. If we work to heal the wound in ourselves and other beings, then this part of the body of the world is also healed."*
> (Joan Halifax)[1]

There is some confusion about how what we call the Four Noble Truths became the central icon of Buddhist teachings. The Truths are found in two versions in the *Dhammacakkappavattana Sutta*, the "Sutra or Discourse of the Great Turning of the Wheel." This text claims to contain the first sermon the Buddha gave after his great awakening.

Many critics can and do point to textual inconsistencies as evidence the Truths were actually woven out of earlier materials. And most scholars believe the Four Truths didn't become normative until as late as the fifth century of our common era.

Buddhism is a vast and complex tradition, and finding a single summation of the Buddhist way and teachings can be difficult. Still, today, all schools of Buddhism agree that the Four Truths are foundational observations of Buddhism. It is significant they appear in the text that purports to be the first sermon the Buddha preached.

First. Human suffering, anguish, angst (*Dukkha* in Sanskrit). This is that visceral noticing of some disquiet that haunts us all. It

---

[1] Joan Halifax, *The Fruitful Darkness: A Journey through Buddhist Practice and Tribal Wisdom* (Grove Press, 2004), 14.

points to the sorrow that haunts human existence. It is not having what we want, and not wanting what we have. This disquiet is a sense of dis-ease that shadows human life. More broadly, it's the tension of all existence.

Second. We are composed of parts in constant motion. In truth we're constantly being created and destroyed. While these "parts" are all insubstantial, our human minds perceive each moment in motion as if it were solid. When we hold too tightly (*Samudaya* in Sanskrit) onto that which is constantly changing we experience this disequilibrium. It's the ultimate fallacy of our organizing brains. It serves us in many ways, but ultimately betrays us.

Third. The good news that we need not suffer this way (*Nirodha* in Sanskrit). It is within our capacity to break the cycles of clinging and suffering. As some say, pain is unavoidable. But suffering, certainly the worst suffering, is optional.

Fourth. The path, the middle way (*Marga* in Sanskrit). Usually this is called the Eight-fold Path of Liberation. There is technical language: Right, correct, profitable View, Right Resolve, Right Speech, Right Conduct, Right Livelihood, Right Effort, Right Mindfulness, and Right Concentration. I've found it very helpful to divide these eight aspects into three parts: The middle way consists of Wisdom, Morality and Meditation. We'll return to this.

Sometimes this description of pervasive human dis-ease can easily be understood as a plain assertion that life itself is suffering. As the second of the truths points out, suffering comes about from clinging. Well, the solution seems pretty obvious. Do not cling to anything. And there's an easy slide from there. Not clinging to anything means not caring about anything.

Gore Vidal in his novel, *Creation*, has the Buddha always gazing into the middle distance, never actually engaging. I've met Buddhists who think this is in fact the point of the Four Truths, including some monastics, and the odd Zen teacher. However, for many Buddhists, and especially Zen Buddhists, as we unpack our disquiet, something different appears. And with that, different solutions to the fundamental problem appear.

What the Buddha taught that is critical for us to understand is that everything, any "thing," and this includes you and me, we're all impermanent. There are no abiding substances, everything is created by causes and conditions flowing together and then breaking apart, creating new things. And, this is so important, that coming together is for a moment. It's all in motion. I've come to call this motion, especially as we experience it: the buzz.

Our human sense of disquiet arises out of the buzz as a side effect of our wonderful human ability to notice and distinguish. The side effect of our noticing and distinguishing is to reify. That is, to make what we've perceived and distinguished something "permanent." What we might think of as real, in the sense of abiding. When, of course, everything really, is dynamic.

Everything is constantly forming and living and dying. And nothing and no one is ever permanent. The buzz is the background noise of existence. For us as human beings what seems naturally to follow our grasping on to what is passing, holding too tightly that which of its nature is in motion. Is hurt. Dis-ease. It's that abiding disquiet.

And. And. The good news is not a list of how to not care, but rather a middle way. Middle way, not in the sense of splitting the differences, but in finding the liminal between. In this sense here between thinking only motion exists, or that things and people have eternal substance. Instead, the Middle Way finds us tumbling into a larger and mysteriously healing view.

In fact, this is more than a view, it is a new way of living. It's sometimes called enlightenment. I prefer awakening. It's always there. It's the natural of the natural perennial. Our original ancestor saw it under the African sun. Our Buddhist ancestor saw it in the foothills of the Himalayas. It has been noticed from every corner of the world.

The perennial we see is a beautiful dance of creation, where we rise and fall together, where our love matters because it is our giving full attention to the precious and passing. It becomes a sort of unknowing, or not knowing, because our sense of self and other are loosened, and we experience each other's joy and sorrow as our joy and sorrow.

And with that shift life takes on an aspect more important than words like "meaning" or "meaninglessness" can touch. These turn out to be sticky words that we cling to. But which only increase our hurt. We find ourselves trapped in an echo chamber of our own creation.

The Buddha offered this teaching to help us through. And Zen teachers and other ancestors manifested out of that teaching ways for us to find this place. The eight-fold path. Me, I can never hold the eight steps in my mind. But I can understand when they're divided into three of those aspects of awakening: Wisdom. Morality. The Meditation. Really, the Path itself.

First. Wisdom is our nondual insight (*Prajñā* in Sanskrit). We see that world which includes each of us as we rise and fall but in the same instance know it is boundless. We see beyond the snares of our imaginations.

Second. Morality is our walking a path of harmony (Śīla in Sanskrit). Sometimes it is rules that hold us together, sometimes it is a description of our awakening itself. It is found written on our hearts, and yet has a life beyond our fears and desires.

And Third. Meditation (*Samādhi* in Sanskrit), those practices of presence that allow us to see our sense of separateness is useful but not ultimately true. The wisdom of sitting down, shutting up, and paying attention. The technologies of the spiritual life. We will be returning to these great gifts in more detail.

So, the Four Noble Truths. Truths? Really good ideas? Working hypotheses? Perhaps an assertion and an invitation.

FIVE HUNDRED LIVES

Exit, pursued by a bear.
(William Shakespeare)[1]

In much of the Buddhist tradition the problem of suffering is connected to a worldview where our human lives continue over near endless time. And the solution to this suffering is the ending of those many rebirths, an extinction of an individual consciousness.

For many this goes right to the heart of the Buddha's presentation, and is found in most short bullet-point summations of the Four Truths. The first question for a critical listener is whether there is in fact a succession of rebirths. Do I survive my death and become another person, or animal, or plant, or rock?

Many Zen Buddhists past and present accept what might be thought of as the traditional understanding that there is a succession of births and deaths on the way to realization and liberation. However, it is not necessary to believe this literally to engage the teachings in a meaningful way.

This point is important to our particular time. Here where we are invited into seeing the natural world and to find the methods of testing and falsification as critical to understanding the world and ourselves. Anyone who looks at any evidence for rebirths or reincarnation offered by those who defend the position, find it hard to ignore how they are all suspect.[2]

---

[1] *The Winter's Tale*, Act III, scene 3.
[2] One of the most intriguing investigation of claims of reincarnation is Ian Stevenson's *Twenty Cases Suggestive of Reincarnation* (University of Virginia Press, 1980). For a critical challenge to this work as illustrative of the issues go to https://skepticalinquirer.org/1994/09/empirical-evidence-for-reincarnation-examin-

And beyond the shakiness of any proof, there's another problem. What is presented as the strongest evidence of rebirths or reincarnation, do not seem to support the Buddhist narratives, where our thoughts and actions result in these specific rebirths. In the examples a good person does not seem to be rewarded in the supposed second life, nor a bad person punished. At best the evidence mostly on offer seems only to show someone maybe has what might be partial memories of a previous life.

Whatever.

I suggest the lens with which to approach all of this is through nondual eyes. The exact mechanisms are not the point. The point is what we find. We need to keep returning to that foundational insight of our mysterious identity. Doors open when we see ourselves in each other and the great world.

Here is what Buddhism offers at the core of its teachings. The axioms of the way, what we need to understand. First, everything is impermanent, rising and falling in causal relationships. Second, that there is no abiding substance to anything or anyone. Third, humans experience this disequilibrium as hurt, or dread. And forth, there is a way of liberation, of peace.[3]

What is truly interesting is that whichever story one embraces, multiple lives or one, or that the multiple lives do happen, but all within our one life, these four axioms remain, and the practices are the same. And—this is critical—the great goal from a Zen stance can be described as ceasing the cycle of lives. It can be described as found in our full-on presence to the unfolding mystery in our moment. Yours or mine.

This introduction to Zen is written from the perspective that multiple rebirths in an objective sense is not a given. But the

---

ing-stevensons-most-impressive-case/ There have, of course, been rejoinders to this rejoinder.

[3] For greater detail of the formulation of the Four Seals as an alternative formulation to the Four Noble Truths, see Dzongsar Jamyang Khyentse, *What Makes You Not a Buddhist?* (Shambhala, 2008).

important thing is: does this accurately point to the currents of our individual hearts? Then we see the power of that story and find ourselves in the project of alleviating suffering in this passing strange life. With that, let's look at what rebirth and karma can look like from an engaged Zen perspective. What follows is one of the central teaching stories of the Zen way. It's all about rebirth and liberation.

Somewhere at the beginning of the ninth century, in China, at a brief flowering during the long decline of the great Tang dynasty, Emperor Xianzong was reconsolidating power, engaging one after another the military governors who had come to rule much of the empire. On the one hand it was a violent and dangerous time. On the other, it was a time of arts and poetry and deep spiritual practice, which resulted in an amazing spiritual literature that today is enriching the whole world.

In this moment a story arose. There's history in it, and it's a ghost story. It sings of the true, the nearly true, and the great dream world. Because of its direct pointing, it's retold all the time. Me, I've lost count of my personal retellings. This little story lives in my heart. It tells me a lot about myself. And by the end of the story, the secrets of the universe, certainly our human corner of the universe, are put on public display.

Including what is awakening in Zen.

In those days, beautiful and terrible, the abbot Baizhang Huaihai, called Baizhang for the mountain in which his monastery was nestled, was one of the greats of an emerging Zen way. He helped to shape what would be transmitted for the next thousand years. His monastic rule would become the standard for the community.

Fiercely committed to a life of meditation and work as being two facets of the way, he lived by the precept "a day of no work is a day of no eating." Sometime after this story his health began to fail. When his monks, worrying for him, hid his gardening tools, he sat at the meal and refused to eat. His rake was returned before the next meal. Baizhang was a fierce teacher of a way pointing to the power of this life we all share, the human way, the way of the wise heart. I count him as one of my heroes and one of my teachers.

I also believe he has things to say to you and me, as we try to find the liberal way in religion, what I consider another facet of that path of the wise heart. He offers a complement to our own attempts at being authentic, at being present and being fully engaged.

Now, with someone as important in the history of a spiritual tradition as Baizhang, well, history and myth, of course, intertwine. And so it is with this story. The abbot was in the habit of giving a talk that was open to anyone, whether a monk, a nun, or just someone in the neighborhood. At some point he noticed within the congregation an old man who had something peculiar about him, like an aura, but of what sort, Baizhang couldn't say. The old man would always stand near the back of the assembly and vanish before the abbot could speak with him.

Finally, one day, the old man lingered and Baizhang said to him, "Who are you, or is it what are you? And why are you coming here?" The old man smiled thinly, bowed and said, "You're very perceptive. I am in fact not a human being. Many ages ago I was abbot on this mountain, heading an assembly of monks following the way." Now, it's worth noticing that would mean as abbot on the same mountain, even if a thousand years before, the ghost was also an "Abbot Baizhang." The old man continued. He said, "A sincere student of the way came to me and asked if someone who had awakened to her true nature, who saw clearly the play of life and death, and had achieved wisdom, was that person bound by the laws of cause and effect, or not?"

"And," asked Baizhang, "what did you say?" The old man shuddered. "I said such a person is not bound by the laws of cause and effect."

There was a horrific silence that felt like endless suffering. Baizhang thought perhaps he smelled the whiff of sulfur. Finally, the old man added, "And ever since then I've been reincarnating as a fox spirit. So far, five hundred times." You need to understand a fox spirit in ancient China is a bad thing, a malevolent being, very dangerous. Big time bad karma.

The ghost leaned close to Baizhang, his breath smelling of rotten flesh, Baizhang could see his eyes had no whites and his teeth weren't human, but razor sharp, like a fox's. "Please," the spirit begged, "say a turning word, and free me from this hell."

A turning word. I think probably we've all encountered such a thing in our lives. A friend says something; maybe we even read it somewhere. Maybe we had heard it a thousand times before, but this time we get it, really get it. And, from that our lives shift, and we go in a new direction. It's part of the human mystery that we have a hand in our destiny, we can make decisions, we can change course.

Baizhang didn't hesitate. He replied, "The true person of the way, she or he who has achieved wisdom, is at one with the laws of cause and effect." Another translation of these words says, "that person does not avoid the laws." And another says, "the wise person does not obscure the laws." Don't obscure, do not avoid, be at one with.

It was as if a bubble popped. With nothing at all changing, the world was now different, now new. Have you had this experience in something small or large? It is a gift. We don't find it by asserting, but by opening. Sometimes people call it grace. The ghost made bows, exclaiming that he had truly heard, truly understood, and this was his last incarnation as a fox spirit. He then added, "My body lies on the side of this mountain. Would you please find it and give me a monk's funeral?" Baizhang agreed and the fox spirit disappeared, that sulfurous smell gone. Instead, there was a lingering odor of sweet grass.

The abbot called for his assistant and told him to announce to the community that after the noon meal there would be a monastic funeral. When they heard this, the monks were confused. One said, "No one's in the infirmary, what does this mean?" But they lived under rule and after the meal they all followed the old abbot. He walked out of the monastery and on until he came to a spot where he took his staff and poked about and prodded out the corpse of a fox. They returned and gave the fox a suitable funeral, burning the body and scattering the ashes.

That evening Baizhang told his assembly the whole story. His senior student Huangbo stood up and said, "Sir, what if the old abbot had given the right answer every time? What would have happened then?" Baizhang smiled, fingering his teacher's stick, and said, "Come here Huangbo, and I'll tell you."

Here's a dangerous moment. If a somewhat different danger than between the fox and Baizhang, to encounter a Zen teacher with a stick in his or her hand.

Huangbo would become another of the teachers who created what we call Zen. According to traditional sources he was a giant of a man, standing nearly seven feet tall, while his teacher was barely five feet, short even for those days. When the younger monk walked up to his teacher, just before coming face to face and just out of reach from his teacher's stick, Huangbo reached out and slapped the old abbot.

Now, up to this moment, perhaps you have a sense of the point to be found in this story, the moral, as it were. But what do you do with this part? I have a friend who has studied this way for many years who can't get past the violent images in many Zen stories, shouts, shoves, and slaps. My suggestion here, again, is that the answer isn't going to be found if we chose to know what's what and to impose something on the encounter. Let it be, as one teacher suggests. Just put it all down, allow that maybe there's a point for us, for me, for you, if we, just for a moment, allow what is to be. Remember grace. It comes unbidden, but mainly it comes to those who are open rather than closed.

As for Baizhang, the old abbot laughed and laughed, and declared, "They say the barbarian has a red beard, but here's a red-bearded barbarian." This is not quite as obscure as perhaps that sounds. The red-bearded barbarian is the founder of Zen, Bodhidharma; a barbarian because he came from India and anyone not from China is a barbarian, and red-bearded, well, because he had a red beard. Here's a simple declaration of delight at his student, and a suggestion of how wisdom was being presented to the whole assembly, an invitation to a deeper stance than merely a nod to moral conventions.

Okay. This is a Zen story. It's what's called a *koan*. A koan is a direct pointing to reality together with an invitation to our own most intimate demonstration of how we understand the matter. In formal koan introspection practice, there are five points to unravel within this story, and for some, six. For our purposes, let's talk about two. First, let's look at that turning phrase about responsibility and our place in the universe. And then, just a little about that concluding encounter turning on the question, "Well, what if the correct answer was given each time?"

Suitable questions not only for Zen monks in ancient China, but also, just as much for us, today. I suggest. I strongly suggest, critical questions for people seeking the ways of the wise heart, a full-bodied encounter with this world, allowing us to walk with some grace upon this good earth.

What is cause and effect? It is understood many ways in different traditions and cultures, but essentially, across cultures, I suggest we find two points. The first is how things relate, one thing, or usually a number, sometime many, cause something. Literally, cause and effect. And this relates to us as much as anything else. You and I are moments in a great play of events. A metaphor we like is how we're all bound together in a web of intimacy. The point is, everything is connected. And out of that realization we see how everything counts. Every action, every thought has consequences.

So, a caution for us. And several invitations.

Pay attention and do good, is sound advice. But this is not just a lesson from a Methodist Sunday school, as genuinely powerful as that might be. I sincerely mean no disrespect to what might be learned in that Sunday school. But there's a further invitation to be found in that last bit—the conversation with the slap and the laugh. Frankly it's what makes this something interesting for me, and perhaps for you: It is an invitation to a life of delight in this world of tears.

We're being invited into a deep ecology, the great earth household. An invitation is being extended for us to see how our lives are so intimately interconnected that what one does, affects what each of us will be. Here's a secret consequence of that truth, we're all going to be reborn as foxes. There is no escape from this life, there is no purity beyond the mess; there is no place we can stand where we will not be splattered with mud from the road.

Here we find we're called to the ways of that wise heart, where we see how each and every one of us is precious beyond description as we are, and our very existence is inextricably bound up with everyone and everything else. The text calls us to who we really are. The true person of the way, she or he who has achieved wisdom, does not avoid, does not obscure, but rather is at one with the laws of cause and effect.

If we know this from our bones and marrow then grace dances into our lives and we will find ourselves transformed, and the fox and the human and the mountains and the great ocean and the vast skies, and you and I, become more intimate than even our dreams can ever say. One family. One life.

That's what it's about. That's what we're about. Nothing less.

TEN OX HERDING PICTURES

> *This is not just a matter of sensing the oneness of the universe. Stars of a tropical sky spread across the ceiling of my mind, and the cool wind unlocks my ear.*
> (Robert Aitken)[1]

So, where does this all take us?

In the twelfth century a Chinese Zen master, Kuoan Shiyuan, wrote a series of poems describing the arc of the spiritual life, and how we move from our disquiet into the great wisdom. He composed these poems as comments on a popular series of images describing that path as a child noticing the footprints of an ox in the dirt and who then begins a journey of discovery.

In Kuoan's poems the whole way of Zen's starting point is described.

> Wandering alone the child searches
> Rising waters, distant mountains, a winding path
> Exhausted, despairing, no idea of where to step
> She hears evening cicadas singing among the maples.[2]

He. She. They. It's important to remember this is a story. Another

---
[1] Robert Aitken, *The Mind of Clover: Essays in Zen Buddhist Ethics* (North Point Press, 1984), 170.
[2] Kuoan Shiyuan, Ten Ox Herding Pictures, author's version.

of those stories that arise from the mystery. It is a story that's about you. Me. It's about our path from hurt and suffering, from disquiet to a deep insight into who we really are. And too what we can be.

Here we get the great beginning of all spiritual journeys. It always starts with noticing something is wrong. Someone has been kidnapped. A magic jewel has disappeared. Here we can go back to the Buddha's great noticing in the first of the Four Noble Truths. Human anxiety. Dread. Disquiet. But we also see in this verse the unique perspective of China and the Zen way.

The girl, the boy hears those cicadas singing in the evening.

The great lists and profound analysis of India comes to China and becomes cicadas calling to us. Analysis becomes poetry. Deep intimations become songs. The Zen way is learning a dance. And the only way to learn, of course, is to do.

The next four verses capture aspects of that dance, that journey sung to us by the ancestors. The verses address when one looks at the various disciplines of Zen, the spiritual technologies of Zen. It doesn't so much describe the details of those practices. We will here, but in a bit. First, however, the feeling quality of those practices. What do they bring us to? What do they show about us that's always been there?

All this, when taken together, brings us to the sixth Ox Herding picture.

> Riding the ox, she winds her way home
> Clothed in evening mists, even the tune of the
>   flute wafts away
> Singing and beating time, joyful
> Now among those who have found the intimate

Then the following three poems describe the dynamic qualities of Zen's awakening. In the Ox Herding Pictures, they're a continuation of awakening, into ever further depths. I suggest we can take each of them as complete in themselves. And when we take them all together, we find how our human awakening is now this, now that.

But in the order of the poems, the first of the deep insights accessible to each of us described on the great way sings of an empty circle.

> Everything empty. Whip. Rope. Human. Ox.
> Who can encompass the map of heaven?
> In the flame of the furnace no flake of snow lasts
> When this is found, the spirit of ancient wisdom arises

Buddhism speaks of emptiness, and sometimes extinction. Here all categories collapse. It is empty. But in Zen that emptiness becomes boundless. The things of the world, whip, rope, human, and ox, are empty. But empty in the very act of presenting.

And this is not the end of the matter.

A next image takes us to a scene of nature. We find the emptiness of things and discover it is boundless. And out of that universes explode, oceans form, mountains rise, and rivers course through valleys.

> Returning to the source, of course even those words a false step
> Better to stay at home, the senses blocked, no effort
> Sitting happily within a small hut
> Look! Running streams. Red flowers.

And even this is not the end. Not in the Zen way. Where the mysteries that can be described as form and emptiness become blood and bone. Out of the boundless rising out of the Great Rift we emerge. In our own time, in our own dreaming, we look up to the early morning sky and we see. The morning star kissing the moon.

Our lives become miracles. Our ordinary actions become the stuff of myth. We get up. We follow the needs of our bodies. We sip coffee and we go to work.

> Without adornment, returning to the market
> Clothed in ashes and mud, with a broad smile
> No need for miracles
> She touches. And dead trees bloom into life

She. He. They.

Our ordinariness, our brokenness, the stuff of our disquiet becomes songs of joy and tunes to which we can dance.

The way and its power. The dynamic we can awaken to.

AN EMPTY WORLD

I am larger, better than I thought,
I did not know I held so much goodness.
(Walt Whitman)[1]

Continuing to dig into what this field awakening is—and why it is so important. And what I personally have found to be at the heart of our common encounter, the perennial within the natural. One of the most important lines in Zen texts is found in the middle of the *Heart Sutra*.

The Heart Sutra is a spiritual text closely associated with Zen. It is chanted every day in a Zen monastery and frequently at other Zen gatherings. It is part of a larger commentarial Buddhist literature called the *Prajnaparamita* cycle. The literature of great wisdom. It is an apophatic literature, that is, it attempts to point to the true by addressing what the true is not. Lots of not this and not that in the Prajnaparamita.

One thing I personally love about the Heart Sutra is that its origins are controversial, at least in some corners of the academic community. There are a number of Buddhist texts in Chinese that do not have Sanskrit or Pali originals and are commonly believed to be apocryphal. That is, texts composed in China and not in one of the two canonical languages. (There is at least one more such language, but what survives are fragments and with no living tradition following.) There is a Sanskrit version of the Heart Sutra. But in 1992 the widely respected academic Jan Nattier

---

[1] From "Song of the Open Road," stanza 5, in *Leaves of Grass*.

suggested the Sanskrit Heart Sutra was in fact a back-translation from the Chinese. Since then, the independent scholar Jayarava Attwood has followed this thesis in considerable, and to me, compelling detail.

The arguments within the scholarly community are not settled. And at this moment the back translation is a minority view. But I am intrigued, and frankly delighted by the idea this central text is Chinese. What it is absolutely, whatever its origins however, is Zen. And at its heart is an assertion.

"Form is emptiness, emptiness is form."

To someone uninformed by the literature of Mahayana Buddhism, or specifically Zen, it is two abstractions juxtaposed. Form. Emptiness. And then Form is emptiness. But also, emptiness is form. This is the metaphysical foundation pointing to the way of insight, to Zen's awakening experience. And I find it true, as I understand such things. And as an expression of nondual reality, this is a very important teaching. But it is also abstract, arid, distant.

However, as we live into what it points to, in the heart experience of it all, I find it compellingly presented as another of those classic lines from Zen's literature. "You are not it, but in truth it is you."

This is a line within the poem, "Jewel Mirror Samadhi." I find it captures the vitality of what the Heart Sutra calls form and emptiness. It suggests just how alive this really is, and with it, us. Me. You. Form. Emptiness. We are revealed as constantly veiling and unveiling mysteries.

The Jewel Mirror is commonly attributed to Dongshan Liangjie, a ninth century Chan master and founder of the Caodong (Soto in Japanese) school. Dongshan is also credited with the poetic map of awakening's faces, his interlocking poems called the *Five Ranks*. So Chinese insight top to bottom.

We are not it, but in truth we are it. You are not it, but in truth it is you. I am not it, but in truth it is me. In a very true sense, it is impersonal in the same way as form and emptiness and their identity. Pointers to understanding the rhythms of the universe. And, it sings right to the core of our beings a truth as intimate as our jugular vein, we, you, me.

Visceral, visceral. Intimate, intimate. This is where the awakening happens. In this messy, animal, and alive place.

For me there is a guideline here. It invites me into the mystery of life, into the dance of who and what we are. Perhaps you sense this as well?

I am not it. My ideas. My desires. My hurt. My longing. My joy. I feel I own them. But I'm wrong. In another sense they own me. These things, ideas, desire, hurt, longing, joy all play out as me, and my part of the great web of things. Now this. Now that. Now a great surrender, where neither quite sings the song right.

So, truth as something inviting. And with that in the poem, "in truth." That's a phrase that does not occur in most English versions. But I've been told by more scholarly friends it is very much there in the Chinese original. I find that important. Even if it becomes a comma or a semi-colon, "in truth" is a moment of turning. The ah-ha. A realization. The great lacuna within which all things birth and die and are reborn something new. Truth. A lovely word. It is felt. It is there. Here.

It is you. As intimate as can be. And me, right to the bones. And the words collapse in the flame of the real.

Voltaire once said, "God is a circle whose center is everywhere and circumference nowhere." Another line that could be added to that collection if we take our word "scripture" as widely as it should be taken.

That. This. You are not God. But, in truth, in truth, God is you. The secret of the nondual. The secret of our lives. In some way I knew this from before I could memorize a phrase from a scripture. It is ancient wisdom. It's what our first ancestor saw as she looked up. It is a truth that is identical to the molecules in my body. Yours.

Intimacy.

Of course, this is the invitation of the spiritual way, in all its different flavors. The hidden and constantly revealed intimate can also be seen as a sort of universalism. We may wander for a lifetime in quest of this intimate thing. But far away or nearer than near, if we're just a little lucky, we find it. And then when we find this intimate truth as ours, we immediately return to the world. Like Dorothy carried away in a balloon, waking from a dream into a dream.

With this gift from the universe, we wander freely. Within the constraints of our actual lived lives, we are free. This brings a good word to this hurting world. We reach out a hand as we can. We are the infinite itself. But we are just this moment, with all the limitations being a moment brings with it.

Form is boundless. The boundless is this particular thing. We are not it. But in truth. It is us. It is you. It is me.

The secret teachings of the Zen way. In the palm of a hand.

SO, IS ZEN A RELIGION?

> *"The emperor closely questioned Bodhidharma. He asked, 'What is the first principle of the ancient way? Bodhidharma replied, 'Vast emptiness. Nothing holy.' Shocked, the emperor demanded, 'Who are you standing here?' Bodhidharma replied, 'I do not know.' Finding no accord, Bodhidharma crossed the river and left the country. Later the emperor took up this matter with his advisor. 'Do you know who that was?' asked his advisor. 'I do not know,' replied the emperor. His advisor said, 'That was the living manifestation of compassion, carrying the seal of wisdom. Filled with regret the emperor wanted to recall the venerable. His advisor said 'There's no point in sending for him. If everyone in the country asked for him to return, he would not.'*
> (Blue Cliff Record)[1]

The word religion is itself a construct of relatively recent western thinkers and scholars. That doesn't mean it lacks usefulness. In fact, the whole point of the word is its usefulness. Investigating what religion might mean has led people on a quest to unravel those parts of a culture concerned with meaning and purpose.

---

[1] Case 1 and Book of Equanimity, Case 2, author's version.

Digging around, things have been uncovered that before the word was coined were obscured. As I've suggested, the broadest use of that word religion is to describe the various means of cultural reinforcement. This sense of religion tells us where we came from and where we're going. It tells us who the family is, and who is not part of the family. Or, really, some idea of family. That's the work of religion most of the time.

And when it is not used to club people who don't belong, it is more than worthy. We are born out of our cultures, our cultures give us language, and tell us much about what we are. The problem is that the negatives, especially the parts that exist to define and to control, loom large. Now in times where we can easily see beyond the strictures of our received traditions, increasingly we're walking away.

But there's more to this that is positive. There's also religion as the songs of the ancestors about hurt and loss, about healing and finding. Often it is about that elusive dream of slumber and waking. It's related to the cultural thing, but runs even deeper. It is the spiritual that people sense and want to extract from the ruin of religion.

Here we find amazing things. The method sounds easy. When we loosen the chains of literalisms, but still take the matter seriously, we can discover amazing things within the collected teachings of any of the world's religions. This can give us that nondual lens, a way to see through the ancient stories, our own intimate lives. This not literalizing is difficult. But a rich project, and a worthy one. Letting go of the religion that is all about right and wrong, while taking it all seriously is no mean feat. And. Doing this we can find what the ancestors wanted to share with us that really matters.

Taking it all as seriously as a heart attack. Engaging everything as an invitation in the secret workings of the world and our own hearts. What does that look like?

Some years ago, I served on the membership committee of the American Zen Teachers Association. It had been formed largely out of a list of names compiled by some of that second generation of Zen teachers, including luminaries like Bernie Glassman and Mel Weitsman. But as it grew, we found it important to explore whether a potential candidate fit the definition of "peer." As a peer support group that was very important.

Anyway, we also found it important to try and clean up that original membership list. And so it came to pass that one of our Zen teachers was assigned to check in with a Roman Catholic nun, Sister Elaine MacInnes. Actually, she's one of the more legendary figures on the Zen scene. While she lived much of her life in Japan and the Philippines, she was a Canadian, and in her retirement was back home in Toronto. The interviewer is one of the more respected among our contemporary Zen teachers. Many would use the word Zen master to describe him. He went to visit. And when he reported back, he said she turned the meeting into a Zen encounter and, well, she won.

So, a Christian Zen master. But also, most Zen masters train in Buddhist monasteries. Some live in them for the whole of their lives. Others become priests in charge of Buddhist temples. Ruth Fuller Sasaki, probably the first Westerner to be ordained a Rinzai Zen priest, co-author of the magisterial study of the Zen koan, *Zen Dust*, wrote a widely read pamphlet, "Zen: A Religion."

While on the other hand the SanboZen roshi, Koun Yamada, emphatically and on more than one occasion insisted that Zen is not a religion. He never phrased it precisely like this, but he very much was pointing to the spiritual within religions.

Part of the problem is semantic. It's how one defines that word "religion." Zen turns out to work for people of no particular faith. It works for humanists. It works for agnostics and atheists. It works for Jews, and Christians, and Muslims. So. Sensei Sasaki is right. Zen is a religion in several senses. So. Roshi Yamada is right. Zen has nothing to do with religions in any of its senses.

In that story of Bodhidharma and the emperor we are told the great way is vast emptiness and that nothing is holy. The central point is not knowing. He's also said to be the bodhisattva of compassion. So, would you say the answer to the question, "Is Zen a religion?" might be, "Yes? No?"

We might say Zen can be the spiritual within religions. Certainly, Zen offers the way to find that spiritual which shows us meaning in a meaningless world.

PART THREE
THE WAYS OF ZEN

In addition to a way of seeing the nature of things and of ourselves, Zen offers specific tools. The spiritual technologies of the Zen way are a particular gift. They've been used successfully for generations. And today, they are being adapted by people from many spiritual traditions, as well as by people of no tradition in particular.

ZEN'S MYSTIC HEART

Oh, Zen meditation of the Mahayana,
to this the highest praise!
Devotion, repentance, training,
the many paramitas –
All have their source in zazen.
Those who try zazen even once,
wipe away beginningless crimes.
(Hakuin Ekaku)[1]

In popular culture the word Zen is often used to mean "space out," or, more positively, to get "into the zone." Whatever that zone is. Here's the deal, or a big part of it. Zen is not about calm nor focus. It does not focus on nothing. Although it does not ignore nothing, either.

Part of the interesting thing is how Zen or more correctly, Chan (Zen being the Japanese pronunciation of Chan), emerged in early medieval China. There the hard logic of Indian scholastic Buddhism gave way to a poetic stance, one of metaphor and indirection. Instead of long sermons and minute logic, Zen became all about pointing and inviting.

The word Zen literally means meditation.

Zen is a way of awakening. And Zen is a way filled with practices. And it has more than its fair share of long sermons and minute logic.

---

[1] Hakuin Ekaku, Zen Liturgy, Empty Moon Zen Liturgy Book, np, 2023, 11. https://www.emptymoonzen.org/wp-content/uploads/2023/09/EMZ-General-Liturgy-5th-Edition.pdf.

These things are not separate.

One Zen master of the thirteenth century, Japanese teacher Eihei Dogen, spoke of "practiceawakening."

The Zen tradition is pretty adamant there is no space between the open and the phenomenal. Just angles of perceiving aspects of reality. Something, perhaps, like waves and particles. Not that I claim to understand waves and particles. But I have sat in Zen meditation a lot and for many years, and this I can tell you: Much of Buddhism the religion is about escape. Natural as natural can be. We intuit the problem of human hurt, and like any animal caught in a trap we seek to escape. But, Zen, despite appearances, the analysis, the disciplines, is about no escape.

It's not just Buddhism that's used to avoid rather than meet. Religion tends to be about escape. Most religions turn away from the world. They seek heavens or they seek hells. People are complicated and often perverse. They, okay, we seek something somewhere else. Even when there's all those stories about seekers of treasure only finding it when they return home and dig in their own basement. While providing good tools for that digging in the basement, Zen retains the whole house. Even the attic with the bewildered and misshapened relative.

Zen offers a way of no escape. Instead, it turns our attention to what is actually here. Here, a wonderful word, here. Filled with wonders. Animals and creatures that maybe aren't animals are all around us, waiting to be noticed.

What is the animal we catch at the corner of our eye? What is the dream that keeps returning, but that when we wake, we can't quite recall? What is the thing about religion that is not crowd control? What is the mystic heart that calls us all wherever or whenever we have come? What is it that takes a hundred thousand million shapes?

Let me offer some possibilities.

Zen is something crazy for this world. It opens doors to the magical real. And with that, Zen challenges how we live in this world, this magically real world.

Zen is about our hearts. And the dark knowing of our hearts. It doesn't ignore the facts of the world, but it does notice how mutable these things are. Zen allows everything a place. Including us. You and me.

Zen is a way of intimacy.

It is about how we live in this world, no other place, this world. It is about the moment, this moment, not some other moment, this moment. And with that it points to who we really are. And, in this world of birthing and dying, what might yet be born.

Perhaps this is a description of your own life as it turns to the intimate.

SIT DOWN AND BECOME BUDDHA

"Sit down and become Buddha."
(Hashimoto Eko)[1]

There are three critical ancient meditation manuals within the Zen tradition.[2] They are based on older texts not specifically Zen. And have spawned numerous manuals since then. Each is worth a deep dive.

But for here, beyond noting they exist, here's a very brief composite summation, focused on the basics you need to begin a Zen meditation practice.

First, prepare yourself by taking care of the body. When you start it's good to wear comfortable clothing. Clean clothing is universally recommended. Next, find a suitable place to sit. Where that is depends. Maybe it's a corner of the room set aside for the practice, as best one can. Maybe it's a local Zen community that you can get to easily enough.

There's more. Of course. These are the foundations for your practice. The throughline is moderation and attention. Clean space. Clean person. As best you can. It sets an intention.

With that the baseline of the actual practice of Zen meditation really boils down to three things. Sit down. Shut up. Pay attention.

---

[1] Dosho Port, *Keep Me in Your Heart a While: The Haunting Zen of Dainin Katagiri* (Wisdom Publications, 2009), 46.
[2] Changlu Zongze, Models for Sitting Meditation, c. 1100 CE. Eihei Dogen, Universally Recommended Instructions for Zazen, 1227 CE. Keizan Jokin, Instructions on How to Do Pure Meditation, before 1325 CE.

First, sitting down.

Now, the Buddha himself taught there were four postures for meditation, sitting down, standing up, lying down, and walking. Each has its place, and each of us will find a closer affinity with one or another. That said, for most of us sitting down is going to be the best thing to do, both to start and to maintain a regular practice. And in the Zen community sitting meditation is where we always start.

Then there is how to hold your body, what to do with your legs, what to do with your torso, and what to do with your hands and head and eyes.

In Zen as it is derived from Japan (and "Zen" has become the preferred name regardless of the national origin of the Zen community), one uses two pillows. The first is a small round pillow called in Japanese a zafu, which lifts the bottom a few inches above the ground. And also a larger flat pillow a couple of feet square called a zabuton. The zafu rests on the zabuton which then protects your resting knees and feet. Place the zafu to the back end of the zabuton. If you sit to the front half of the zafu your crossed legs will naturally incline to the surface of the zabuton. It is important to work toward getting at least a single knee to the zabuton.

And, obviously, one need not run out and purchase pillows. Folded blankest can do just fine. At least as you're beginning.

The ideal position is called a full lotus, where the feet rest on the thighs. With stretching and over time, many people can do this. It is the most stable of positions. With the bottom raised by the zafu and the knees both dropped to the ground, a solid triangular base is created. The half lotus with one foot on the thigh is slightly less stable but works fine. Resting one foot on a calf is called the quarter lotus, or in my circles, the half-ass lotus. Setting one foot resting in front of the other, but with both the knees to the ground, is called Burmese. They all work.

Other options include kneeling, by either sitting on a sidewise zafu to take pressure off the ankles, or using a kneeling bench, called a seiza bench for the same effect. Some use computer chairs, which naturally creates the same base. And, finally, one may sit in a chair. We'll look at chairs a little more later.

The secret here, as with all these positions, is to have the bottom slightly higher than the knees. This creates that triangular base. Most people who are serious about the practice, unless there is a significant physical obstacle, find getting on the floor the best thing.

Of course, this is just establishing the base for seated meditation. The idea is to sit with an erect and upright posture. We do this by holding the back straight, by which we mean the natural "s" cure of the human upright posture. Resting comfortably on that triangular base, a slight push at the small of the back, together with holding the shoulders back slightly should reveal what upright looks and feels like. If you don't feel comfortably upright swaying the torso back and forth or in shrinking circles will take you to that centered and upright position.

If you tuck your chin in slightly and mentally align your ears with your torso, your head will be resting comfortably upright. Place your hands in your lap, placing your left hand in your right, allowing the thumbs to touch lightly, creating an oval. This is called the "cosmic mudra." Pull your elbows out slightly. In Zen meditation one sits with the eyes open, with the gaze falling forward to the floor a couple of feet ahead.

If you're just present, noticing, but not following the thoughts and feelings as they rise, this is called *zazen*, meaning seated Zen. And sometimes it's called "just sitting" (*Shinkantaza* in Japanese).

Of course, few of us are just sitting. We worry about the past. We plan for the future. It's an amazing field where stories arise, some very hard to ignore. So, when beginning the practice most teachers encourage some slight intervention to help with concentration. There are a number of methods including counting and sometimes mantras.

I recommend one of the simplest of the forms. Take five breath cycles and put a number on each inhalation and exhalation. So, one on the in breath. Two on the out breath. And so on until ten. Then start over again.

Just breathe naturally. The posture will encourage diaphragmatic breathing, filling the lungs from the bottom. But just let this happen naturally. And if it doesn't, don't worry. Even with all this, the mind still wanders. When you notice, as you inevitably will, that you've lost count, just return to one. If you discover you've slipped into a robotic counting and are at twenty-six, just return to one.

The catch is, rather than returning to one we often feel a need to place blame somewhere. The two basic directions are inside and out. We notice we've lost count, and we blame ourselves, not good enough, not smart enough, too much bad karma from a previous life. Of course, what has just happened is that instead of noticing and returning we've entered a meta-distraction. Just come back to one. Others prefer to blame the environment, if it wasn't for my neighbor's grumbly tummy, if it wasn't for the kids playing upstairs, if it wasn't for the traffic outside. Same meta-distraction, just pointed in a new direction. Return to one.

There's a third distraction that can be even more seductive: "But this is a good idea." The solution to some problem, the plot for the great American novel, or just a deeply satisfying train of thought. The deal is you've committed to this practice for a brief period of time. In Zen the number ranges from fifty minutes down to twenty-five. If the thought is really that important it will return. Come back to one.

Think of the practice as "olly olly oxen free." Come home, come home, all is forgiven.

Just sitting. Just this.

Intimate. Intimate.

A baseline practice is probably about half an hour a day most every day. Serious practitioners usually sit more, often a lot more. But you will notice this practice touching your heart if you can maintain that half hour a day, most days.

An occasional retreat, half day, full day, two, three, five or seven days can be enormously enriching. For many of us, this is a critical element to the discipline. And we do what we can.

At first, just getting your bottom on the pillow regularly is all that is required. If you hope to develop a real practice, at the beginning regularity is vastly more important than duration. Five or ten minutes a day three days a week done consistently is way more important than setting an intention to sit two hours a day and not doing it.

There are a number of strategies that help. It helps to sit at the same time each day. They say the morning is golden and the evening silver, but in truth, whatever time of day you can do consistently is best. Sitting in the same place each day is helpful, if you can. And if you can reserve the space, creating a small shrine or something that marks it out for this purpose can be helpful. All these are strategies, and not to add to the burden. Do what you can, as you can.

A NOTE ON THE USE OF CHAIRS

I praise the chair as a spiritual aid. A chair is a tool for sitting in, a gift invented and produced by human beings for human beings. This body knows how to sit in a chair. There's a lovely geometry to a person in a chair, with the legs, seat, and back of the living body parallel to the legs, seat, and back of the chair, in a double zigzag, expressing the rightness of right angles.
(Susan Moon)[1]

I have been practicing Zen well past fifty years. My skin is wrinkling. My hair is a different color than it was in my youth and maturity. Many of my male friends have little or no hair. I'm shorter than I once was, by as much as two inches. And I need to go to the bathroom when I need to go to the bathroom. Admittedly, I still am not worried about buying green bananas. But I know that day is right around the corner.

I'm in a new season. And there are new ways of focus. And practice.

Each of the moments in our lives invite new perspectives. For example, I love that ancient anthology of spiritual anecdote and direction, the *Blue Cliff Record*, Case 36:

---

[1] Susan Moon, "Leaving the Lotus Position," *Tricycle*, Winter 2008.

> One day Changsha went off to wander in the mountains. When he returned, the temple director met him at the gate and asked, "So, where have you been?" Changsha replied, "I've been strolling about in the hills." "Which way did you go?" "I went out following the scented grasses and came back chasing the falling flowers." The director smiled. "That's exactly the feeling of spring." Changsha, agreed, adding, "It's better than autumn dew falling on lotuses."

Now, the way the whole thing is presented is so perfect. A radical call into the way. There is a path, but we need to wander, and being in its general vicinity is enough. Following those scented grasses. Returning chasing the falling flowers. Each step full.

And. Then there's that observation about the spring feeling. There is something glorious as we tumble into the way. Especially, if, like spring, it is so full of promise. Genuinely wonder, genuinely wonderful.

But really, autumn dew falling is just as intimate. Less future in front of it. And, maybe with more aches and pains. But. Without doubt. Genuinely wonderful.

Also, this case reminds us, while we're constantly called to this moment, it is also a journey. We are mutable. And passing. And we are constantly invited to notice. Every step is golden. Going out. Coming back. Mysteries unfold.

These days when I sit in meditation, I almost always sit in a chair. After decades sitting on the floor in the traditional style of the Zen way, I've found the power of just sitting in a chair. Over those earlier years, when for one reason or another I've had to sit in chairs, I felt embarrassed. Sort of like I was cheating. Or, as a teacher that I was setting a bad example. I was mistaken.

For a number of reasons, not least because the early Zen

meditation manuals pretty much always talk about sitting on the floor in a full lotus, with the only concession to human frailty in a half-lotus, many Zen teachers tend to ignore, make light of, or discourage sitting in chairs.

There is a legitimate question about pain. Pain is a feature of sitting for long periods of time, especially cross-legged on the floor. A certain level of pain just comes with being alive, and being obsessed about some pain is missing a great deal of what Zen is about. But there is understanding pain, dealing with pain, and there is romancing pain. Zen is not about fetishizing pain. Or, rather shouldn't be.

As to fetishes. I know one Zen teacher who told me he didn't like how chairs affected the aesthetic of the line of meditators. Some fetishize the posture, saying that it is the identity of practice and awakening, as if no other thing is the identity of practice and awakening. A sad literalizing of a deep truth. We need to find that place where our bodies and our awakening are not two. Thinking it means a specific posture is that miss which is as good as a mile.

And, while I've at least had the decency never to tell anyone they had to sit on the floor cross-legged, I did hold myself to that rule. For many years. But times change. Bodies change. And, and this is important, sometimes we never have the option of sitting cross-legged on the floor. The autumn dew falling on lotuses. No better. No lesser.

The Zen teacher Susan Moon notes, "There are plenty of challenges to chair sitting, so don't worry that it's too easy—you can still be miserable. The five hindrances of lust, sloth, ill will, restlessness, and doubt assault me in a chair as easily as they did when I sat on the floor. Pain visits me, too, on occasion, sharp and hot between the shoulder blades, but I know it's not injuring me, and it doesn't stay."[2]

We're being called into an intimate moment. Zafu. Chair.

---

[2] Moon, ibid.

Heck, I've found some of my best moments have been sitting in my rocking chair.

And here's a fact. Chair sitting is going to be increasingly a part of my practice. And, here's another fact. It is perfect just as it is. Just being present. Just breathing. Each breath can be the last. Just as each breath can be the first. Opening our hearts, opening my heart, each breath a wonder.

And another small lesson. Learned over and over. Turns out one of the blessings of the autumn practice is how it is mostly about letting go.

Letting go. Really letting go. And, how that is just fine.

TAKING A WALK ON THE WILD SIDE

> *"We should go forth on the shortest walk, perchance, in the spirit of undying adventure, never to return – prepared to send back our embalmed hearts only as relics to our desolate kingdoms."*
> (Henry David Thoreau)[1]

I have friends who suggest to me how anything they really like doing is a meditation. Often, they're just being cute or ironic because they know this is one of those things floating around the shallower ends of the spiritual world that annoy me.

When someone is saying this sincerely, the principle they seem to rely on is that such things as knitting, bowling, cooking, all involve concentration. And, at best, an achieving of a sense of oneness with the object of their concentration. And, true enough. I have little argument with such an observation.

Indeed, many of the so-called Zen arts such as tea ceremony and archery are such joining of action and attention. And they can be worthy projects, great supports to the larger disciplines of meditation. And practical extensions of the meditative practices into ordinary life.

Now that my spouse Jan and I live in Los Angeles, in the land of near continuous sunshine, we've taken up walking. At first on a near daily basis. Of late a tad more haphazard. I notice

---

[1] Henry David Thoreau, from "Walking," first published in 1862 in *The Atlantic*.

even here how one of the hallmarks of a sincere spiritual practice is regularity. It is something we cherish. It started out mostly as a health thing. And it remains that. But it has something else going on about it, as well. I'm finding something that is a traditional form of Zen meditation, but something tweaked and made a bit more indigenous to the West.

The most traditional form of walking meditation I encountered as I began to practice was *kinhin*. Kinhin is done between periods of seated meditation. It can be as little as five minutes. And it can be for an entire period. In other forms of Buddhist meditation walking can be a major part of the discipline. Special tracks to walk are often a part of those disciplines.

Walking is something we all have to do, as long as we have the means to do it. At some point we may arrive at a place where walking itself is difficult. Many, maybe most of us who are lucky enough to live long enough, may discover walking ceases to be a possibility. So, the very act of walking is from the beginning an invitation into gratitude.

From there we can notice the miracles of it. Of how we're supported. How the earth and the air and the many smells as we move, each are invitations into the moment in all its wonder and mystery. Perhaps, with just a little luck, we notice each step becomes a miracle.

It's good to walk slowly. To notice your forward motion is in fact a falling forward. To discover how your breath can connect to the step can be a powerful experience. As you lift the foot and notice, both the mechanics of your walking, and the beauty of it all is revealed. As you move the foot forward new worlds are revealed. As your foot comes back to the ground it can be the meeting of heaven and earth. Even as an openhearted knitting or bowling or cooking might do the trick, yes, very much, walking is the way.

The shape of the practice may or maybe not be a little more

difficult than just sitting down, shutting up, and paying attention. But ultimately it is just walking.

I suggest trying a variation of that ancient practice. A way that might be considered part of our emerging western forms of Zen practice, where we mostly are householders. And where our ordinary lives are the container.

The Unitarian Transcendentalist Henry David Thoreau's primary spiritual discipline appears to have been "sauntering." It sure looks a lot like this openness to reality that is at the heart of Zen sitting, an authentic objectless meditation practice. His essay "Walking," was Thoreau's focused reflection on sauntering as a spiritual discipline. He also points out what comes to us when we let go of our expectations, hopes, and fears. Near the end of that essay Thoreau writes, "We walked in so pure and bright a light, gilding the withered grass and leaves, so softly and serenely bright, I thought I had never bathed in such a golden flood, without a ripple or a murmur to it. The west side of every wood and rising ground gleamed like the boundary of Elysium, and the sun on our backs seemed like a gentle herdsman driving us home at evening."

Any Zen practitioner will recognize the words. Certainly, what they point to.

A traditional Buddhist approach to walking meditation is to find a suitable path; it can either be a simple quiet place that you can walk back and forth on, or it can go someplace. Destinations are not quite the point. And a place where you can walk back and forth eliminates the need to attend to many possible distractions.

It's good if you can walk barefoot.

Walk upright as best you can. Let your gaze fall forward. Some like to let the eyelids fall halfway closed. Generally, one walks more slowly than ordinarily.

Let the mind settle into the body, then bring your attention to your feet. Be aware of the parts of the feet as you move.

Sometimes it's helpful to mentally label each action, stepping. Or labeling raising the foot. Then. Labeling setting the foot down.

The point in traditional disciplines is bare attention. So eventually you stop labeling.

The Vietnamese Buddhist meditation teacher and social activist Thich Nhat Hanh invited three points to consider in taking up walking as a meditation discipline. I describe them as setting an intention, notice your environment with gratitude, and then bringing mindfulness of breathing and mindfulness of walking together.

Or. You can breathe in. Notice. Breath out. Notice. Pay attention to your body and environment. Repeat.

Or. You can saunter. Just take off. In town. On the beach. In the mountains.

Begin walking. Saunter. Notice.

When you notice the mind has wandered away from the walk, come back. Resume your saunter.

At the end of his essay on walking meditation, Thoreau sums it all up by returning to the image of walking toward the Holy Land. "So, we saunter toward the Holy Land, till one day the sun shall shine more brightly than e'er he has done, shall perchance shine into tour minds and hearts, and light up our whole lives with a great awakening light, as warm and serene and golden as on a bankside in autumn."

BREATHING ZEN

"One breath taken completely; one poem, fully written, fully read—in such a moment, anything can happen."
(Jane Hirshfield)[1]

In my particular corner of the Zen world, when one is giving basic meditation instruction, once the body is addressed, we turn to what to do with the mind. Most commonly breath counting is considered the first step. Counting the breath allows one to develop a little concentration. This helps the beginner to keep focus and when, as it does, the mind wanders, breath counting allows a quick way back to the moment at hand.

The fact that we're going to breathe anyway gives us something to touch, to be aware of with minimal distraction. And so, attaching numbers to the breath is a skillful means. But there are other aspects to the breath and its possible connection to the larger meditative project that's worth noting.

It also anchors us at that place where body and mind most clearly connect. As such it is potentially a very important thing. In the Rinzai school this is much more emphasized. But whatever school of Zen one finds most resonance with, it's important to remember how important the breath is in the mind-body connection. More than simply a useful way to keep us returning to the moment.

Japanese Rinzai practice is grounded in a breath discipline

---

[1] Jane Hirshfield, *Nine Gates: Entering the Mind of Poetry* (Harper Perennial, 1998), 41.

taught by the eighteenth-century reformer of that school, Hakuin Ekaku. He taught Zen meditation's foundation as "counting the breath meditation."[2]

It is not necessary to believe in Chinese metaphysics to discover the value of using your breath in meditation.[3] In modern physics a center of gravity is an imaginary point in a body where the weight of that body centers. Even if imaginary, it has actual real-world consequences. The human body also has these imaginal centers of gravity. Dancers and actors can move the sense of centeredness throughout the body with consequences to how they occupy their role, their sense of balance, and how others see them.

There are consequences in our physical lives depending on where we place our consciousness, where we find or place our center of gravity. Whatever one's beliefs about Chinese metaphysical and medical theories, there are immediate psychophysical reactions when we visualize our life energy and "place" it at the center of our being.

After finding a balanced posture, you simply feel the cycle of your own breath, inhalation and exhalation as a whole. Being aware of the breath anchored at the center where it begins and ends, where it starts and to where it returns. It's abdominal breathing, but with the addition of feeling your consciousness resting there in your center.

The Rinzai master Shodo Harada speaks of six stages of counting the breath practice. A form of a six-stage model of practice traces at least as far back as the *Abhidharma*, dating from

---

[2] *Susokukan*, "counting the breath practice."
[3] There are three technical terms, *ki*, *tanden*, and *hara* used when considering breath in Chinese meditation. Ki is the Japanese rendition of the Chinese term Qi. Qi is a central concept in East Asian thinking with applications in religion, medicine, and martial arts. Often ki is seen as the life-source, or life-energy. This energy is believed to flow through all things including our bodies. Tanden, or Hara, can be understood as the center. The use can be complicated, but for here the tanden or hara is the imaginal center of a human being. It is believed to be located about three fingers beneath the navel in the middle of the body.

perhaps a hundred years after the death of the Buddha and the earliest attempt at organizing his teachings.

Later, a sixth century Chinese meditation manual by master Zhiyi, *Six Gates the Sublime,* provides the basis that would continue to develop within the Rinzai school. Counting the breath practice is a sort of map with instructions. In this case the first two parts are physical practices while the subsequent four describe your interior experiences. These help you to know whether you're on track or not.

The first stage is simply to count the breath. Usually, a full cycle inhalation and exhalation count as "one." Then the next full cycle as "two." Three. Four. And so on to ten. In this it's not much different than the Soto style, except there's the clear instruction to put the focus of consciousness at the center of our being.

The second stage is simply being aware of your breathing, in and out. It all becomes a harmonic whole. Emphasizing and finding the oneness of the experience. Or, really, beginning to notice the oneness of the experience. This unfolds over time. By breathing from the tanden, it's easier to come to the experience of that oneness of breath.

The third stage is stopping—not stopping the breathing itself, but where your mind stops discriminating about what is this and what is other. Here you are simply aware of the unity of your breath and your body. Not exactly one, but not two. Just letting the breath roll on as part of a greater whole that is the body mind. Experiencing it.

At the fourth stage, you move to being aware of how this unity informing the multiplicity of things extends to everywhere. At this point the difference in the rising and falling of the breath is not really experienced within the body nor outside of the body. With an attenuated center sometimes noticed, sometimes not. Now the center is no longer simply an "I." But rather, it's as if the universe itself is breathing. The center is just noticing.

Next at the fifth stage, the focus turns inward again, but from this much broader perspective. Here this broad field of possibility is like a light that can be turned inward. Here we can dig into that multiplicity of things as one thing. We can experience our individual lives more fully, as rising and falling. Our thoughts, our history, our feelings, rising and falling within something vastly larger.

Here the mind body becomes a field of possibility. Felt. Experienced. Without judgment or anxiety.

And finally at the sixth stage, all sense of self and other fall away. Feeling. Experiencing. Without self, without other. Here we understand the term "just this" as vastly broader and deeper than what concerns our egos.

But there's a beginning to this. Counting the breath practice points to an arc of possibility. So, paying a bit more attention to the awareness of our breath and our breathing at the beginning can pay off in some very interesting ways. It doesn't matter if we believe in Chinese models of the universe. Just let your imagination and your breath do their work.

Focus your attention at your center of gravity: placed, felt, found, at the center. Your exhalation should be long and steady. At first when you feel the natural end of the exhalation, it's important to push a little farther, completely emptying the lungs. Soon this extended outbreath becomes much more natural.

Here, the extended outbreath is zazen. Zen meditation.

That the first stage includes counting is important. Awakening just happens. It is like the fabled spirit that lands where it wills. But there are things we can do to invite the spirit. This counting focuses the mind and being to train it to not be trapped by thoughts or feelings and to be more receptive to larger possibilities.

While counting to ten is the most common practice here, there are any number of possible variations. None of which is wrong.

Tips along the way include trying to avoid making the counting mechanical, slipping into automatic counting. I recall counting to ten once. Then I found myself hitting thirty-two. To be clear, this robotic counting is not what we're trying to do. The standard advice applies whenever we have lost our way. Notice that it has happened, and then return to one. No side trips. No blaming self or other.

Just notice and then promptly back to one.

Simply counting the breath as an anchor to concentration is an easier practice to begin. It's harder to grow into this deeper and more focused breath practice outside of a controlled environment like a retreat. But it can be done.

As with any spiritual practice the point is to continue, to bring your heart to the matter.

And then again. And then again.

Mysteries await.

SAMADHI

> *A student of the intimate asked the master Huguo, "What about when every drop of water has become ice?" The master replied, "It will be shameful once the sun has arisen."*
> (Book of Serenity)[1]

The heart of Zen meditation, what makes it go, is samadhi.

Unfortunately, or maybe fortunately, samadhi is a slippery term. But, slippery or not, it's important to have a sense of what it is. The word *samadhi* comes from the Sanskrit and is most commonly translated as concentration. In a bottom-line sense samadhi is a word for different states of openness. It is a field of consciousness, a place of preparedness and willingness.

It is a term common to all the Dharmic traditions, that is the religions of the Indian subcontinent. And with that there are nuances of meaning that differ among the schools. In Hinduism as presented in the spiritual classic the *Yoga Sutras of Patanjali*, samadhi is the culmination state found at the end of many mental steps. Some scholars see a rough analogy in Patanjali's samadhi states to Pali Buddhism's several Dhyana states of absorption. It's worth noting the Chinese pronunciation of dhyana is Chan, while in Japanese it's rendered Zen.

In one sense samadhi is found through the investigation of bodily sensations and mental actions, which naturally allows the

---
[1] Book of Serenity, case 28. Author's version.

meditator to let go of unhealthy mental states. What remains is a field of consciousness marked by equanimity and bliss. And this is samadhi as the word is generally used in Zen.

While something of a gross simplification of an often-mysterious place to rest the human heart, I offer it as a pointer. But even here the what and the how of samadhi has multiple facets.

For instance, the thirteenth-century founder of Soto Zen in Japan, Eihei Dogen, in his "Bendowa" fascicle described a "samadhi of self-fulfillment." Which is perhaps best unpacked in another fascicle, the *Genjokoan*. Here's the place the various disciplines of meditation take us to. And specifically shows the approach of Zen meditation.

"To study the buddha way is to study the Self; to study the Self is to forget the self; to forget the self is to be enlightened by myriad dharmas; to be enlightened by myriad dharmas is to drop off the body and mind of self and others."[2] In other translations myriad dharmas is rendered the ten thousand things. The many expressions of this wildly emerging, presenting, and dying world.

And, this is important, samadhi isn't the point of it all. Rather it is a place we can find in human consciousness where the universe, the real, can present viscerally. A common term for this is unmediated. But as everything is mediated, we experience the world through our six senses, and then create stories to understand what we experience. Samadhi is a place where the stories don't grab us by the throat. It is a place where the stories can shatter. And deeper truths can be discerned.

So, it's important. Samadhi sets the stage. It is not awakening. It foretells the wonder that is possible. It foreshadows. Basically, it prepares the place where wonders might birth. In a sense, samadhi is a way of seeing the world that prepares us for the intimate experiences, the fundamental shifting of perspective that is awakening.

---

[2] Shohaku Okumura and Taigen Daniel Leighton, *Master Dogen's Zazen Meditation Handbook* (Tuttle, 2022), 45.

Much of Zen practice as a technique opens the mind in important ways. The contemporary Rinzai teacher, Meido Moore, describes samadhi "generally as a relaxed, sustained stability within which the mind functions freely without fixation or distraction."[3] Our habitual dualisms are loosened within samadhi. This allows what is, to come to us. And critically, it predisposes us to those illuminating moments in which the world and our hearts can shift. These encounters, awakenings, what in Zen are usually called *kensho*, our seeing into the nature of things in a way that shifts the ground, making who we are new.

And arriving at this place of preparedness, of openness, is the goal of samadhi. Zen is about awakening. The shattering of our delusive perspective on what is. Samadhi is our allowing ourselves, gifting ourselves, preparing ourselves for our encounters with awakening.

It's also important to note how both samadhi and awakening can be deep or shallow. With many possible problems. Among them it's possible to mistake samadhi for awakening. Samadhi states feel good, and sometimes people get attached to samadhi. There's a term of art, "samadhi junky." I find myself thinking of one of the people who are thought to have more meditation experience than almost anyone else. He could and often did slip directly in samadhi, and stay there. But his ordinary life was a disaster. His need to experience samadhi left him unable to function in any other way. An extreme example of missing the point, but a real one.

It's also a common mistake for us is to take a small glimmer and think it's the enlightenment of the Buddha witnessing the rising morning star. Well. In a sense any awakening is that, is the Buddha's awakening. As they say a drop of water and the ocean are both water. And there are slight glimmers and oceans. This is

---

[3] Meido Moore, *Hidden Zen: Practices for Sudden Awakening and Embodied Realization* (Shambhala, 2020), 27.

part of why the Zen teacher Joko Beck was extremely reluctant to call these disruptions of our heart's perspectives as kensho, but rather universally she used the term "small intimation."

It's wise to approach all this with some humility. It's also a good idea to have a guide or guides along this way. To help find our way into samadhi and to discern what happens there. A competent guide helps us sort out our experiences, and in the Zen way, tests them.

Sometimes I prefer the term, "field of possibility," instead of samadhi. I use field of possibility for several reasons. One, because these states of openness, of non-clinging, are not necessarily found within formal meditation. This is important. We're probably more likely to have our awakenings, the disruptions or shattering of our misconceptions within samadhi, or closely associated with samadhi. And so, a great deal of the Zen project is focused on cultivating this mind of possibility.

At the same time those possibilities are there as part of our natural human inheritance. People wake up when and how people wake up. From the first ancestor, possibly near the Olduvai Gorge, looking up into the sky and seeing the morning star kiss the moon, people have been waking up. Field of possibility implies at the very least other fields.

One example from the *Abhidharma* is the samadhi of the eight-fold path. Because simply embracing the path of meditation and wisdom and the ethical container of harmony is itself a field of awakening.

Another is the moment-by-moment samadhi. In the traditional literature we find *khanika samadhi*, which is the samadhi or everyday life. In our Zen life I suggest this is where we most commonly encounter those disruptions of our habitual ways of seeing the world and ourselves.

There's the wonderful story about Chinyo. She was a thirteenth-century Japanese lay monastic, really a servant in a convent. With only the rudiments of instruction, and without regular access to the meditation hall, she applied the principles to her regular life, her moment-by-moment life. Then one day she was carrying a bucket of water. It was night but the moon was full, and she walked along with that illumination. She could see the moon reflected in the water within the bucket. The bucket was old and the bamboo strips that held it together were beginning to pull apart. She may or may not have been aware of how fragile it was. Then all of a sudden, in a moment faster than a breath, the whole thing fell apart. The water splashed everywhere.

And. Well. A small intimation.

As she was illiterate, she had to ask someone else to record her description of that moment. She recited:

> With this and that I tried to keep the bucket together,
> And then the bottom fell out.
> Where water does not collect,
> The moon does not dwell.[4]

Awakening is when the ordinary and the miraculous are not two.

I have little doubt that a strong practice opens us to these possible moments. And moment by moment, the moment is presenting. Waiting. Sometimes. Calling us. Often. Maybe always. And if we give ourselves to the project, if we allow ourselves to be present, then both traditional meditation on the pillow with all the disciplines associated, and these moment-by-moment samadhis we experience when we pause and pay attention, each can and do reveal the mystery.

Wandering around the spiritual bazaar that was the San Francisco Bay area in the late 1960s, and reading what was

---

[4] Florence Caplow and Susan Moon, *The Hidden Lamp: Stories from Twenty-five Centuries of Awakened Women* (Wisdom Publications, 2013), 37–38.

available, through a combination of good luck and mysterious karma, I stumbled on a book, *Zen Flesh, Zen Bones*, by Nyogen Senzaki and Paul Reps.

The book, or more precisely the section called "Centering," offered me my first practical instruction on what moment-by-moment samadhi might look like. At least it provided instructions that made some sense to me.

It was simply a list of 112 pointers for meditation.

In his foreword to the book, Reps said this section was from a living practice in parts of India, but that it could have been as much as 4,000 years old. He also claimed it could be the root of Zen. It was actually the *Vigyan Bhairav Tantra*, a chapter from the *Rudrayamala Tantra*. It's framed as a dialogue between Shiva and his consort Shakti, where Shiva offers those 112 pointers. It probably was composed between the seventh and eighth centuries of our common era in Kashmir. Today there are several translations available in English.

Maybe not a source for Zen, but definitely from the same deep root.

When I was first learning the arts of meditation, they were useful to me. Especially those early pointers connected to the breath. Later, I realized they each pointed to samadhi moments. They were invitations into fields of possibility, moments pregnant with our awakening. They showed where and how a moment-by-moment samadhi can be encountered.

Among the things I really found useful about them was their emphasis on ordinary moments in our lives, a couple even addressing sexual acts. When I read it, this was tantalizing.

Here I offer ten of the 112 pointers, framed out of my own experiences:

1. At the moment the breath turns, inhalation and exhalation: notice. When we're able to

notice the passing parts as well as their more concrete expressions, the unity of our lives begins to reveal itself.

2. As your lover touches you, be only the touch. Your hand on the beloved can feel like electricity. Allow yourself to drop into the moment, let go of the next stroke of the hand. Be only this expression, and that expression becomes the sun and the moon and the stars.

3. When driving, be one with the rhythms of motion. Don't shut off any sense. Be present to the bounce of the car and movement of other cars around you. Feel the sky rushing by. Just flow.

4. When looking at some ordinary object, experience it as if for the first time. When I was a child, I turned over the page of the Sunday comics and wondered what it would be like to witness the page for the first time. I let it happen.

5. Look up at the blue sky. Just gaze. Just notice. Allow it all, don't close down the horizon.

6. Repeat a word. Om. Mu. Amida. Jesus. Enter the sound. Feel it shape in your mouth and your head. Let go of meaning. Just be it.

7. When meeting an old friend, enter the joy. Memories fill us and spill over when we greet an old friend. But it's important to let the memories fade and to meet the person

who is now with you. It is the secret joy of the worlds.

8. When eating or drinking, become one with it, be filled by it. Food is sacred. So many religions use meals as sacred acts. As you eat, pause, notice, savor.
9. When you notice your mind wandering, this moment is it. Instead of blame or regret, notice the moment. It joins the whole universe in the possibility of awakening, in the fact of awakening.
10. At any moment bring your mind and body and breath to it. Each moment is a gift. Just this one. Just this one. Breath into it.

Moment by moment, the deep silences, the field of possibility. Samadhis. Samadhi.

KOAN AND HUATOU

> *"I came to the practice out of a desire to find the intimacy within life, to hear the call and response of this moment, to feel the connection between myself and the world, to find my place in the great way of things. I wished to bridge an essential estrangement I'd felt with my own life. I was drawn to the koan way because I thought it operated outside the known ways of doing things. It seemed to be connected with a knowledge contained inside the immediacy of life."*
> (Rachel Mansfield-Howlett)[1]

It seems we all have a question. Why was I born? What is it all about? Who am I? What is this? I believe such questions co-arise with our becoming human. These questions were articulated at the same time as we created language. Or, perhaps, as language created us.

The exact framing of the question is unique to the individual, as we emerge in our specific time and place. So, for me, in my adolescence along with all the other things of changing body and awareness, I realized how desperately I wanted to know if there was a God.

Is there a God? Every other question, every other longing,

---

[1] Rachel Mansfield-Howlett, "At Home in the World," in James Ishmael Ford and Melissa Myozen Blacker, eds., *The Book of Mu: Essential Writings on Zen's Most Important Koan* (Wisdom Publications, 2011), 207.

was put into that one question. It burned in me in ways that words simply fail to convey. And it drove me on to the spiritual journey, to the great quest of the heart. My heart.

In Zen there are two ways of taking questions as invitations to discoveries, a bit different than what we find in conventional questions and answers. One is the *koan*. The Chinese words *gong an*. Koan literally means "public case," as in a legal document. It is a word, a phrase, a whole story. It is wrestled with, with a spiritual director. And it is explored within the deep places of samadhi. And sometimes it explodes out of our moment-by-moment samadhis.

The other is closely related. *Huatou* is a Chinese word, roughly meaning "word head," or "essential point." I've also seen it rendered as a "critical phrase." The term is *Wato* in Japanese.

In our English usage, the Japanese word koan has become normative, as we came to that practice first with Japanese teachers. While we usually use the Chinese word huatou because it comes to English speakers first with Chinese and Korean teachers. As Ralph Waldo Emerson noted, "a foolish consistency is the hobgoblin of little minds."

Koans arise in early medieval China as a uniquely Zen discipline. The scholar-priest Victor Sogen Hori suggests they arose when Zen monks overheard Taoists playing a drinking game, where someone would spontaneously offer up a line of poetry, which the next person needed to match. Winning and losing was determined by the onlookers. Early Zen teachers saw how this could work as a spiritual discipline when attached to those burning questions of the heart.

They soon saw that the form of the question did not have to arise with the individual. Teachers found they could use phrases derived from conversations among Zen masters and from the masters and their students. Once presented to students of the intimate, these phrases were reflected upon, and what they found would be presented to their spiritual director. Eventually collections were gathered together with commentaries. Some of these collections like the *Wumenquan*, the "Gateless Gate," the *Biyan Lu*, the "Blue Cliff Record," and the *Congrong Lu*, the "Book of Serenity," are now considered treasures of world spiritual literature.

There are crucial points within koans. A koan might contain several points. Sometimes the whole koan might be that point. "Mu," which is the negative response to a question, *"Does a dog have Buddha nature?"*—a response that seems to violate the normative teachings of Mahayana Buddhism, is an example.

They're meditated on and then come together as questions and answers to be met in usually private interviews between a student and a teacher.

In Japan, especially in the school of the eighteenth-century master Hakuin Ekaku, they become curricular, a long list of questions to be met. Each demanding answers. And, yes, right answers. This becomes one of the great gifts of the Zen way, a course in awakening. It offers access into insight, and then, critically, and possibly uniquely among the world's spiritual disciplines, offers extensive direction following those initial insights into the mysteries of our hearts.

Huatou practice is a variation on this practice. As we've said, it's called wato in Japanese. Chinese koan practice followed Dahui Zonggao's teachings. At the end of the eleventh century, Dahui felt koan practice had degenerated into mere examples of literary brilliance. Beautiful. Sometimes dazzling. But no longer a discipline on the path of awakening. He even famously tried to destroy the existing copies of his master Yuanwu Keqin's collection, the *Blue Cliff Record*, as a distraction from the primary point. Fortunately, he failed there.

He offered a reform to the discipline. And this is what we generally call Huatou practice. Huatou can be seen as the original heart of formal koan practice. And through his influence on the Korean master Chinul, the practice we differentiate from koan practice, certainly from curricular koan practice, remains the normative form in both China and Korea.

Huatou are very brief phrases like *What is God?* or *Who am I?* or *What is this?* They're phrases capable of self-emptying, and bringing us along, toward an intimacy that words in and of themselves find elusive.

In my own pre-Zen days, *Is there a God?* burned hot. As I attended to it, I realized that the question wasn't quite right. "Is there a God," was a first draft of my deep question. Somewhere along the line, and I can't say when, or how, the question reframed itself for me. "What is God." In Zen Buddhism the same question, the same passion might be found with the question "What is this?"

The first draft of my personal koan began to reveal itself as too intellectual and had too much to do with falsification. Something important, but not the burning thing. The factuality of God is an important question, and following that thread led me on a path of trying to understand the shape of the world. Actually, it led me to try and understand to some degree the shape of the cosmos and the place of humanity within the cosmos. It was important and I'm grateful for that.

But it wasn't the real question. Not my deepest question. Not the burning question. The real question was what is the mystery? How do I understand this life? Are we just meat? And what is this wonderful and terrible thing that I find everywhere around and in me? God was the placeholder for all of this. Like "What is this?"

Then. For me as I dug deeper, at some point I found the world in which God was no longer even necessary. And with that, the question changed once more. The word almost disappeared. Instead, what I had was a burning curiosity. A wondering.

Today as I try to name it, I see how words fail. They're important. They take us places. But at some point they fall apart. At least when we're looking for the most important thing. That question of meaning and purpose. For me while I could say God, what it became for me was the lens of a telescope or perhaps the lens of a microscope.

If I understand Dahui's reform, it was to worry less about finding a "correct" answer to the koan, and more to find what it showed the student of the way, where it took the practitioner. On my own path it was finding that at the heart of my question was some great doubt. And whether one is following a curricular form of the practice or simply sitting with one question with no expectation, however subtle, there would someday be another.

The secret of the practice is discovering the heart of doubt.

This doubt would take me on a path where I would discover Zen's traditions helpful in ways that settled the great hurt and allowed me a way to live into mystery that was so transformative, that, well, gave me my life. Not precisely the life described in the extravagant descriptions of enlightenment, which too often pretend another place; but as it really is, at one with the highs and lows, at one with knowing and forgetting, at one with successes and failures.

Koan and Huatou are the expressions of intimacy. Using the language of my original question, Koan and Huatou show us how to know God.

The contemporary Chan master Sheng Yen offered a simple three stage description of the Huatou as a practice. It's a good framework.

After being assigned the question, or finding it for oneself, I would add, simply repeat the question. You can think of it as a mantra, a sacred phrase to be chanted or recited or sung. Slowly while paying attention. Analytically, trying to understand it. Then, trying to feel it. Live into it. Let it take over. Let the wandering mind, your wandering mind, focus with the Huatou. In some ways this is a gathering of the mind, a form of concentration.

As it becomes intimate, then drop the question into that intimacy. Find the deep curiosity, the longing. Feel it. Explore that sensation. Allow the question to take that shape beneath or behind or within the Huatou. Notice how it is the same or different. Find the doubt that informs the question. Here the mind expands from concentration and we begin to experience a larger perspective.

From there bring the questioning, the doubt sensation and that larger perspective, that openness of mind together. With this we discover the sense of doubt shifts and mutates. The poet Mary Oliver invites us, "You only have to let the soft animal of your body / love what it loves." The deep curiosity of the heart plays out with and through the Huatou.

At this point in this map the doubt can shatter. And at that point we discover the purpose of our heart.

In curricular koan practice, one takes this practice using a type of koan, what are sometimes called breakthrough koans, such as Mu. And after a time of looking at it from differing angles, to move on to other koans. Although in my experience with Mu, that core of the question; well, we never completely leave it.

In Huatou practice one returns to the question over and over again. It becomes a lifetime touchstone.

In curricular koan practice, one often finds the deeper meaning within the meeting with the spiritual director. Or if not exactly in the meeting, in bringing one's experiences to that meeting. Huatou practice relies less on these interviews, although they are important.

In either case the point is the intimate. Not one. But not two, either.

GREAT DOUBT, FAITH, AND ENERGY

> *"The ancients spoke of three essential conditions for Zen practice: First: Great faith; second: great doubt; third: great determination. These are like the three legs of a tripod."*
> (Koun Yamada)[1]

When I first started Zen practice in the late 1960s, there weren't a lot of books about Zen readily available. Alan Watts's wildly popular *The Way of Zen* was published in 1957. It made the somewhat more abstract work of the scholar D. T. Suzuki accessible, if at the same time suggesting a version of Zen that didn't really touch on practice. But for me, fortunately, by my time there was also Philip Kapleau's collected and published lectures and essays on the actual disciplines of Zen. *The Three Pillars of Zen* was published in 1965.

Perhaps most remembered today for its collection of contemporary awakening experiences, it was also the first book I found that actually addressed both the why of Zen and, critically, the how of pursuing it. In the lecture by Hakuun Yasutani, "The Three Essentials of Zen Practice," I was introduced to the heart of that practical path which is Zen's great gift toward our intimate nondual awakening.

One enters the way, after learning the rudiments of Zen

---
[1] Koun Yamada, *Zen: The Authentic Gate* (Wisdom Publications, 2015), 193.

meditation, whether sitting, perhaps involving the breath, perhaps not, walking, retreats, or through liturgy, any of the several disciplines. The beginner is invited into a personal consideration of life and death and who we really are.

We enter this consideration following three strands: faith, doubt, and energy.

Yasutani Roshi points out that "Buddhism has often been described as both a rational religion and a religion of wisdom. But a religion it is, and what makes it one is this element of faith, without which it is merely philosophy."[2] True. And it's more complicated. I'll return to this. The second, and perhaps most unique aspect of Zen against pretty much all the religious traditions of the world, is doubt. Or, rather, how we engage doubt. Doubt as the great engine of Zen practice. It's more complicated, and I will return to this. And third is great energy. Persistence or determination. It's also more complicated, and I will return to this.

Paying attention to these three things, we find the method of Zen.

These necessary elements were first put together systematically by the thirteenth century Chinese master Gaofeng Yuanmiao.

First is faith.

Faith, or "the great root of faith, or "great determination," as one translation has it, is as if one is "leaning against Mt. Sumeru." Sumeru is the sacred mountain at the center of things. As I take it, it means a confidence experienced when one physically touches a mountain with one's own hands and feet, feeling the incline, noticing the dirt and plants, hearing the swoosh of a bird and perhaps the call of some animal that you can't quite make out.

It's the body-knowing of direct encounter. This is a letting go of the clouds of our minds and experiencing who we, you, and I are on the other side of our stories about ourselves and our

---

[2] Philip Kapleau, ed., *Three Pillars of Zen: Teaching, Practice, and Enlightenment* (Anchor, 2000), 87.

separations. I find a corollary in this in the Japanese term, *shinjin*, as clarity, perhaps as a clarified heart-mind. It's as if the clouds that normally obscure our experience of the world have parted and we see things the way they are.

And the truth is, I don't have that kind of confidence. Faith doesn't come naturally to me. I tend to see calls to faith as calls to blind faith. That is, a statement is delivered from on high, and I'm expected to submit. Not in my nature.

I'm too much a child of the Enlightenment, by which I mean the Enlightenment of the West: naturalistic, materialistic. Claims are subject to testing, measurement, and are subject to falsification. For me, doubt is a very real and constant thing. It both helps me and it builds some unnecessary barriers.

But this Zen faith is different. I know this is true of other faith traditions as well. But I understand it through my Zen experience. It's more a feedback loop of confidence in my own experiences. Guided along by the tradition, I take what native intuition I have about the fundamental matter, encounter it, deepen what it is I've experienced, and proceed on, a sort of cycling down into depth.

Traditionally, throughout the world's religions, doubt is a problem to be overcome. We see this view of doubt in many religions, and in much of Buddhism this is no different. In the Theravada, doubt is considered one of the five hindrances to fully following the way. So, when I saw that Zen considers doubt itself is a strand leading to awakening, I felt invited into the Zen way of intimacy. I found something I could lean into.

Next is doubt.

Doubt I get. There's so much to doubt. The news. Politicians. People. What I think. I look honestly and see very little that I feel should be axiomatic. It all seems subject to change, nothing I seem to own stands up to honest examination. Honesty, of course, is the nut of that problem. It's the easiest thing in the world to lie to ourselves.

So how does this become a spiritual practice, or the juice firing my spiritual practices?

Yuanmiao says of doubt, "the great ball of doubt," or "great indecision-and-apprehension," that it is like one has done something in secret, something shameful, perhaps a crime, and you know you're about to be exposed. Anxiety, a profound dis-ease. It is the existential dread that touches our hearts and sours everything. But now, here on the Zen way, it is also a path into the fundamental matter of who we are.

Faith can be seen as the intuition that everything is right, what might be called the original blessing, the intimation that we are all more intimate than our words allow us to think. Doubt can be seen as the knowing that we are mortal, subject to every failing. And in some very real way, our sense of who we are, in all our failings, is a curtain shading our joys.

One can see how they complement each other, faith and doubt. Faith, or what we find in the exploration of that mountain at the center of the cosmos, is as close to the essential as we're going to find. Although this "essence" in fact is the lack of any abiding substance, it is the pure interaction of all the elements of the universe in constant play, rising and falling, as one thing. As no thing, as in Buddhism it is sometimes said. While doubt is the knowing of our very ordinariness, our fragility, our hesitations, they arise as a dynamic in our hearts. As our hearts.

They are, as natural as they are, the stuff of our awakening. Taken together, things can emerge, can be uncovered, can be experienced. Together they can synergize, and in a sense become one thing. Now faith, now doubt.

Now one thing.

Two threads winding and carrying us forward. Allowing us

to trace along the vermilion thread into mystery. And so, great energy.

Energy, or "the great overpowering will," or "great passionate intention," or "determination of great fury." Energy is easy to comprehend, dedication, purposeful engagement. Wrath is a more interesting translation, evocative of levels of engagement. It's a kind of dynamism. As Yuanmiao tells us, it's as if you've found the person who murdered your father. The feelings that envelope you perhaps wanting to strike him down with a sword wielded with all the force in your being.

As with doubt being treated by images of guilt, I find this thirteenth-century illumination of energy as desire for revenge very helpful. I get it.

In our time and place we have an inclination to smooth things over. In general, I think this is salutary, politeness is the lubricant of society, and decency and good order are worthy in their own rights. But here we are moving into the most desperate of things. And it calls for impolite action, full-hearted, even reckless, desperate action.

Fired by our knowledge something is wrong, we are embarked on a path. One that calls forth everything.

RITUAL AND LITURGY

> *A student of the intimate said to the master Yunmen, "The radiance serenely illumines the whole universe...." Before he finished Yunmen asked, "Aren't those Zhangzhuo's words?" The student replied, "Yes." Yunmen said, "You have misspoken."*
> (Gateless Gate)[1]

Humans do rituals. It's part of our being the symbol-making animal. Fourth of July parades, graduation ceremonies, baptisms and dedications, recognizing a child's coming of age, weddings, funerals, are all rituals. Some are religious in nature, others are not.

We're all familiar with the term "rites of passage," coined by the French ethnographer Arnold Van Gennep in 1909. The rituals of our rites of passage can be critical to our wellbeing, to finding ourselves within our lives.

I spent a quarter century as a Unitarian parish minister. Over the years I've accompanied many families suffering a death among them. What I observed was that those who had a ritual moment acknowledging the loss weathered the time following better than those who did not. Not a certain lock, but a pretty good rule of thumb. There does seem to be something deeply true about our ritual acts being important.

Rituals are part of all religions. A classical definition of ritual structure in religion suggests four elements. It is a repeated

---
[1] Gateless Gate, Case 39, author's version.

action. The celebration of the Christian mass, or offering incense in a Zen temple, for instance. They are set out of regular time. That is, it they're separate from our ordinary actions in some manner. They follow a pattern. And they carry with them a larger story, the myth of the tradition—in some way.

For instance, in the Gateless Gate:

> Once upon a time the world honored one was at Vulture Peak. Before a vast crowd of lay practitioners, nuns, and monks, angelic creatures, and even gods, he held up a single flower and twirled it. Of the assembled crowd only the disciple Mahakashyapa, responded, breaking into a wide grin.[2]

Commenting on this most famous of Zen's sermons and that little act of twirling a flower and smiling, Carl Jung once suggested this is not far from the Mystery of Eleusis when the priest held up a reaped ear of grain. And not unlike the transformed wine and bread presented by the priest at the Christian communion. Or the offering of a stick of incense at a Zen morning liturgy.

I suspect these rituals are all part of that natural perennial. For some, these rites—the ordinary things done with reverence and attention—are spiritual disciplines just as much as sitting in Zen meditation or taking up koan introspection.

Liturgy means "public service," or "the work of the people." Within a Zen context the late John Daido Loori Roshi was fond of saying, "Liturgy makes visible the invisible." Making the invisible visible in Zen means bringing our whole lives together. Liturgy is a symbolic expression of that fullness, which, like zazen, opens us to a way of being in the world. Zen rituals in East

---

[2] Gateless Gate, Case 6, author's version.

Asia focus on the transference of merit. Here we see our ancient desire to be helpful.

Here we find the power of non-separation, the reality of our intimacy with the ten thousand things. Rituals reveal the fundamental truth of our lived mutuality, embodied. Or, can. Engaged with full hearts. And bodies.

Such engagement captures the whole world. All of it. Our lives and our stories collapsed in a moment of noticing. Just this, and from this noticing. From that flower as it twirled. From that smile, that lovely grin. Just as it happened. With an offering of incense and a bow.

Rituals place us in the rounds of life, give us a sense of rightness, including healing hurts. They draw our attention into our sensory experiences, and can inspire us as we live through the vicissitudes of life.

Liturgy and ritual are an important component of communal self-definition. Which is both important and dangerous. Dangerous because, while it reinforces who is "in," it also enforces who is "out." It is a powerful and potentially harmful part of all religions. And if used carefully, it can be one of the most powerful of spiritual practices.

We all have our little and big rituals, which can simply be brushing our teeth in the morning or making a cup of coffee exactly the way we want it. And rituals can be unhealthy. In that big way of cutting other people out, or in a more intimate way, as in an obsessive action. The compulsive acts that are part of the diagnosis of obsessive-compulsive disorder.

There is doing the ritual, getting lost in it, missing the whole point. Yunmen tells the student of the intimate that merely quoting a poem that describes facing into the real is a mistake. What he invites is not ignoring the poem. He is inviting the practitioner to find the real and make the writing and reciting of that poem the student's own.

Rituals small and large, private and communal, are part of how we interact, communicate, both within our inner lives and as members of a society. Zen tradition has evolved a number of rituals to help along the way. There are daily rituals, such as those surrounding meditation, having a particular place, lighting candles, offering incense, concluding with a verse. There are weekly rituals, for many joining with others for meditation once a week is an example. There are seasonal observations. For many, attending retreats at least quarterly. And there are annual observations. The great festivals of Zen such as Rohatsu, marking the enlightenment of the Buddha as our own.

There are ritual acts like eating meals in a formal way.[3] These are powerful disciplines and I'll return to this later. Actually, there are ritual ways of engaging all the daily activities of life.

A connecting thread for rituals of daily life can be the recitation of *gathas*. The word means to speak or sing. In Zen, gathas are brief phrases, perhaps just a word, maybe a verse recited at various moments in the rhythms of our lives. Traditional gathas in the Zen world include the three refuges, the four vows, and a verse recited before putting on the rakusu, a small vestment worn by many Zen practitioners.

But we can have our own gathas, and many people do. A grace at mealtime. Something for when we get up in the morning. Something before we go to bed. Perhaps something for when we are about to use a toilet. Someone suggested to me it might be good to have a gatha before turning on a television set.

Several Zen teachers have shared versions of gathas including Robert Aitken and Thich Nhat Hanh. You can profitably use theirs. You can compose your own. For instance, here are a couple of mine, inspired by Aitken Roshi.

---

[3] *Oryoki* in the Japanese tradition, and *barugongyang* in Korean.

> As I awake, I offer myself into the great project of noticing, of being present.
> As I wash the dishes, I offer my attention to the disciplines of life.
> As I experience anger, I offer a moment to untangle, to notice the heat.
> As I notice birds calling, I offer up my ears.
> As I listen to the news, I offer space.
> As I settle into bed, I offer a moment to feel the quiet.

Collect ancient verses, find collections like Robert Aitken's volume, *Zen Vows for Daily Life*. Discover the rhythms of life and death in these moments.

The radiance serenely illumines the whole universe...

These moments touch the real. They channel the real. They are the real.

LOVINGKINDNESS

"No external condition can prevent love; no one and no thing can stop it. The awakening of love is not bound up in things being a certain way."
(Sharon Salzberg)[1]

The relative isolation of the various Buddhist schools in relation to each other in Asia has gradually unraveled in modernity. Mahayana monks join Theravadins for meditation. Japanese Zen priests travel to Tibetan communities. Academics in the differing traditions attend the same conferences.

On the ground we see the influences of differing traditions on each other in small and larger ways. Nowhere is this more obvious than in the West, where not only is it possible to see influences from non-Zen traditions in Zen communities of practice, but also non-Buddhist influences. For instance, it has become common to see yoga practice in Zen centers.

One aspect of Buddhism writ large, that has seen a growing influence in western Zen, is the embrace of Lovingkindness and its disciplines. Tenzin Gyatso, the fourteenth Dalai Lama famously declared, "My religion is kindness." And there really is something that runs through all our human hearts. Lovingkindness is a religion for all people.

I suspect that impulse to kindness, whether achieved or not, is a deep intuition we share as human beings, constelled with

---
[1] Sharon Salzberg, *Loving-Kindness: The Revolutionary Art of Happiness* (Shambhala, 2002), 29.

love and compassion. When we meet the intimate, our human response usually arises within as that constellation of kindness and compassion and love.

It can be approached in several ways. One of those ways is through intention and practice. Certainly, I feel kindness to be my religious aspiration. At least a significant aspect to it. I believe it is a manifestation of Zen wisdom, one that is too often missed. Zen wisdom as an expression of lovingkindness is a correction to the sometimes dry and abstract expressions we hear.

One wonderful thing is that it need not be merely an aspiration, or an example of self-deception. Kindness is something that we can cultivate.

Lovingkindness (*Metta* in Sanskrit) is one of the three meditative disciplines that Gautama Siddhartha taught. It becomes the foundation, and by learning it we can open ourselves to compassion (*Karuna* in Sanskrit), where we share in the joy of other's successes (*Mudita* in Sanskrit), and finding ourselves looking on all things as they rise and fall with equanimity (*Upekkha* in Sanskrit). Taken together they're called the four abodes, or four abidings. But the foundation for it all is Lovingkindness.

The Lovingkindness Sutta sings out the heart of the practice:

> Even as a mother protects with her life
> Her child, her only child,
> So with a boundless heart
> Should one cherish all living beings;
> Radiating kindness over the entire world:
> Spreading upwards to the skies,
> And downwards to the depths;
> Outwards and unbounded,
> Freed from hatred and ill-will.
> Whether standing or walking, seated or lying
>   down

Free from drowsiness,
One should sustain this recollection.[2]

This is said to be the sublime abiding. In some ways it looks like a form of cognitive therapy, a reorienting of one's attitude. It helps set the troubled heart at rest and creates a frame from which we engage our lives in more healthy ways than perhaps we would otherwise. And, it can have deeper consequences still.

The discipline is simplicity itself.

In most forms this is a self-guided meditation. There are five people who become the imaginative focus of the meditation. First, yourself. Then a benefactor. Think of someone you feel you owe a great deal. Then a friend or a family member. Someone for whom you have abiding affection. After that someone you can picture, but maybe not even name, for whom you have neutral feelings. Perhaps your mail carrier or a clerk in the grocery store you usually go to. And finally, a difficult person, an adversary, perhaps an actual enemy. This is someone who has hurt you in word or deed.

Experienced teachers suggest not to make the objects for this meditation people of the opposite sex, or, if your affection goes toward your own gender identity, that person. As it proceeds the discipline can be quite powerful, and among the distractions of these practices, among the most seductive are what are called "near enemies." A near enemy is like mistaking pity for compassion, a state that resembles but is not the one we are looking for. In this case, the whole thing turns on love. And a powerful near enemy of love is lust. And as the discipline progresses, we can fall into erotic states if we are not careful.

It is all about love. And love is a notoriously elusive term. English is notoriously weak in collapsing so much into that single word. The Greeks had their famous four words for love, naming

---

[2] Karaniya Metta Sutta, trans. Amaravati Sangha, online https://www.accesstoinsight.org/tipitaka/kn/snp/snp.1.08.amar.html.

eros, and fraternal love, and familial love, as well as something "higher," divine love, *agape*.

Love has to do with a constellation of feelings felt for another. Precisely what that means invites a multitude of definitions—as we perhaps know as we consider our many affections. Often, we see lists of what love in Buddhism is not. No clinging is at the heart of it. Lust is not it. Neediness is not it. As to what it is, that's a bit harder.

We've already mentioned lust as a "near enemy." There are so many confusions. Love is about as loaded a term for us as is religion. We need to be careful. My dharma successor Tom Wardle observes how we need to be careful about "the assumption that meditating on love should make you feel more loving. For many, that is the result, often quite immediate, an afterglow of sorts. And that is not everyone's experience. Some practitioners can find Lovingkindness very challenging, emotionally confusing, or even upsetting. It might be worth noting that it isn't all roses with this practice."[3]

Actually, this is true for all these practices. They touch the deepest matter, and therefore are dangerous things. Also, we need to be cautious about anything that seems to guarantee a specific result. I've just not seen it work that way. For this as for any of these practices, they're ancient, they are often effective, and every person meets them differently.

I suggest love, certainly any Buddhist love is found living into the heart of, as the Vietnamese monk Thich Nhat Hanh calls it, our Interbeing. Our deep response to this discovery of our true intimacy on this planet is an experience of love. Sometimes in Buddhism called lovingkindness. I suggest love in Buddhism is the experience of our deepest intimacy with everything else in the world.

---

[3] Personal correspondence.

This experience arises naturally with our realization of who we are. Even when we don't have a conscious understanding of this, it invades our dreams. We are surrounded by intimations of the deeper truths of our reality. But we can also cultivate this, orient our consciousness in the directions of our great hope. Or, when we have achieved some insight, Metta can deepen and broaden its experience. So, while not a traditional Zen practice, Metta can be very important for us. And it is an increasingly common discipline used within Zen circles in the broader West.

Metta is a practice that can and should extend through the whole of our day and night, whether we're formally meditating or in any of the many actions of our lives. Still, it is usually best to introduce it as a sitting meditation practice. For that people are encouraged to find a clean and comfortable to sit. Sitting upright, with your hands resting in your lap or on your knees, breath quietly. Most people close their eyes. Then we marshal three elements, one or all. They are visualization, our imaginative engagement, or contemplation on an object. In this case feelings of good will, or, with our voice, out loud or sub-vocally, when we can reduce the focus to a word like lovingkindness, or even more simply, love.

This is all boiled down to some simple phases. Traditionally they include a wish to be free from danger. A wish to be free of suffering. A wish for happiness. A wish for healing. A wish for peace and for ease. Some lists are a little longer. Others are a bit shorter. One way to phrase it, for that first part, for yourself, might be:

> May I be free from danger. May I be free of suffering. May I be happy. May I be healed. May I find peace and ease in my life.

The invitation is for us to delve deeply into what this might mean. We can do this by visualizing ourselves in these various conditions. Slightly different, we can imaginatively experience that sense of good will and consciously direct itself to our being. And we can reduce this down to those simple words holding implicitly all of it, "free" or "happy" or "peace." Or, love.

This can be explored for an extended period of time. Half an hour. A day. A week.

At some point we move to the next person. Someone who has been important to us, a teacher, a mentor, someone who has helped us in some significant way. "May (name) be free from danger. May (name) be free of suffering. May (name) be happy. May (name) be healed. May (name) find peace and ease in their life."

Again, this can be explored for an extended time, half an hour, a day, a week. It should be the same amount of time you gave to yourself.

The next step is a friend, or perhaps someone in your family. Again, devote the same amount of time you had for yourself and your mentor.

Then push it out to that person you can picture but perhaps not even name, who you know in some sense but for whom you have no strong feelings. Again, wish them well in the same way and for the same amount of time.

Finally, extend it to that person for whom you hold ill-will. Wish them freedom from danger, freedom from suffering, happiness, healing, peace and ease. Again, for the same amount of time you have for everyone else.

And then, repeat.

At first the practice can feel artificial, and resistance to persisting can arise in all sorts of ways. But we are encouraged to continue. Gradually the sense of artifice begins to be replaced with a naturally arising positive regard. And from there, we begin to experience the fruit of the practice.

We are speaking of technologies of the spirit, what in classical

Buddhism are the techniques that allow one to see through the delusions of our ordinary lives to something else. While Metta by itself is not said to awaken us, we can see in its practice the proof of its pudding. Also, it both lays the ground for other disciplines, and clarifies what we can find in those disciplines.

COMMUNITIES OF PRACTICE

The master Baizhang was charged with naming a founding abbot for Mount Daigu. He called his community together and set a full water bottle in their midst. He said, "Don't call this a water bottle. What will you call it?" The head monk responded, "It's not a wooden shoe." Then Baizhang asked the head cook, Guishan, what was his view on the matter? Guishan kicked over the water bottle and returned to his kitchen. Baizhang laughed and sent Guishan to Mount Daigu.

(Gateless Gate)[1]

I strongly recommend finding a community to practice with. I also recommend finding a spiritual director. I'll talk about that later. The ordering here is intentional. I believe most people wishing to take up a practice will quickly, maybe immediately find it is very hard to practice alone, and finding a group to practice with is about as important as taking up the practice itself.

While there are large training centers and even monasteries around the country, most likely you're going to encounter a small or smaller group. It probably will rent space, possibly at a church. There is an old joke that the majority of today's Zen centers

---

[1] Gateless Gate, Case 40, author's version.

were started as groups meeting in the basement of a Unitarian Universalist church somewhere or another.

As you seek a community, what you will encounter is a bit of luck of the draw. And depending on where you live, there will be greater or lesser opportunities. But increasingly it's possible to find a group not terribly far from where you live.

Here I will outline the history of formal Zen training and the monasteries and Japanese temples where Zen was practiced. However there have been a lot of shifts as Zen has come west. And there are differences between types of monastic training and what you'll find in a householder-oriented group. This chapter will also look a little at what communities of practice look like today, and what you're likely to encounter at those places.

Here is where you find the practice of Zen moving from theory to practice. And with that it gets messy. There are monks and nuns, often collectively called monastics. They may or may not be celibate, although increasingly non-celibate clergy are called priests. There are also householder teachers. The communities led by these teachers take different shapes.

When I first started Zen practice in the late 1960s, the San Francisco Zen Center was already a major presence in the Bay Area. What I was not aware of at the time was that there were two communities occupying the same space with the same spiritual leader.

Sokoji temple had been founded in 1934, when the congregation purchased a former synagogue on Bush Street. What I thought of as the Zen Center was actually a guest organization, originally an activity of the temple. When the previous minister, Reverend Hodo Tobase, retired in 1959, he had been succeeded by another Japanese priest, Shunryu Suzuki.

Suzuki had a longtime interest in America and was the first of the temple's ministers to be a fluent English speaker. With the publication of several books about Zen, especially Alan Watts's

1957 best-selling *The Way of Zen*, there was an increasing interest in the subject in the wider community, especially in cosmopolitan enclaves like San Francisco. Reverend Suzuki was the right person in the right place at the right time.

The temple served mostly a Japanese-descent community, and most services were conducted in Japanese. The new people coming were mostly white, and few spoke any Japanese at all. They had been coming in small numbers for some years. But now they had a priest who could communicate with them. What they wanted was meditation practice and a spiritual director.

In 1969, the leadership of Sokoji temple asked for Suzuki Roshi's resignation as their priest. Too much of his time was taken up by the expanding needs of the Zen Center and the growing numbers of students. Dr. Martin Luther King, Jr, once ruefully commented how Sunday morning was the most segregated hour in America. And that was part of it, a cultural and religious divide. But there was something else happening at the same time.

There was a lot I didn't come to understand until later. One was the term "Zen center" and what it meant. As they were officially separating from the temple, they called their project a Zen center rather than a temple or a monastery. Or even a "church." A reasonable option as that term was already being used by the major Japanese derived Pure Land religious community, the Buddhist Churches of America. The name Zen Center was suggested by Robert Hense, and was used when they formally incorporated in 1961. Center was chosen because they were forming a new kind of community. And it needed a name.

By the time I arrived there were already three substantial Zen centers in different lineages around the country. The one in San Francisco, another in Los Angeles, and a third in Rochester, New York. Before many years had passed there would be many more.

While Zen has always had householder practitioners, the normative place to study and practice from when it emerged in

China were within hermitages and monasteries. Sometimes a hermitage would become the locus of an emerging monastery. People would hear of a master trying to live quietly, and gradually people came, hoping to study with that master. And another monastery might arise. More often the hermit would remain hidden from fame and gain, living quietly, and dying alone or perhaps in companionship with one or two students. There may or may not be some kind of succession.

While Zen's literature suggests there were school-specific monasteries, in fact throughout China's history, monasteries were eclectic things. They might have a meditation hall, but they also might have a chanting hall, and a sutra study hall.

People called into the Buddhadharma would ordain with masters of the monastic rule. Some would devote their lives to understanding the nature of the rule and seek liberation within it, while some would devote their lives to the study of ancient texts they'd received from India, and which seemed to keep appearing. Others would feel the call of Amitabha and find a life devoted to calling on the sacred name, while still others might throw their lives into the disciplines of the meditation hall.

Abbots of these monasteries could come from any of these schools. And it was common in Chinese and Taiwanese monasteries for the succeeding abbot to come from yet another school. We can also see something similar in modern Korean Zen, where abbots and masters of Zen practice are usually different tasks.

Householders, for most of Chinese history, were mainly drawn from the scholar bureaucrat class, among the few with leisure time for interests beyond survival. Some visited the monasteries, took up the disciplines of Zen, and on occasion awakened. And sometimes they would even be acknowledged as masters in their own right. A few would even have dharma successors of their own.

But mostly, Zen belonged to the monasteries and hermitages.

Then Zen came to Japan. There Buddhism began to specialize, and what we can think of as specific schools would eventually have their own monastic complexes. So, Zen was first practiced in Japan by monastics from the emergent Tendai school. Tendai very much reflected its Chinese origins, taking a comprehensive view of the dharma, seeing itself as offering a reconciliation of the different approaches.

The earliest Japanese monastics who were attracted to Zen were Tendai monks. Most notable among them were the Rinzai founder Myōan Eisai, and not much later the Soto founder Eihei Dogen. Eisai may never have thought of himself as anything but a Tendai monk.

However, Japanese Buddhism also quickly began to form school-specific monasteries. Dogen, most famously, while rhetorically rejecting sectarianism, was among the first to establish a totally Zen-specific monastery, Eiheiji, in 1244.

Over time, especially after a series of imperial decrees beginning in 1603, Japan instituted what would evolve into denominational structures, with head temples and branches. These branches were smaller and often had one or two resident monks. They came to function as parishes serving the liturgical religious needs of the local community. In effect, monks gradually became parish priests.

Another important aspect to Japanese Buddhism was how, beginning in the ninth century, ordination followed a new system. The vows had a looser formal statement about celibacy. The ordained were understood by the community and by themselves to be monks or nuns. But at least in the case of monks in these temples, many had lifelong companions, usually called housekeepers. And over time there were children. This would come to a head in 1868, when the imperial court removed all criminal penalties for clerical marriage. In the Zen schools, pretty much instantly the vast majority of clerics married.

For many years before the reforms of the nineteenth century, the temples had become largely hereditary. Increasingly what happened is that aspirants to their father's temple were expected to spend a period of formation at the lineage's head temples. Gradually, head monasteries with lifelong members became training temples. While some people would spend their entire lives there, mostly they were seminaries creating priests for the many thousands of local temples.

The San Francisco Zen Center became the paradigm of the next major shift. The people coming to study with him were there specifically to learn the practices and to grow deep with them. What that meant in practice was there was no way these practitioners were going to go to established temples. Instead, it was once again all about practice.

In the thirteenth century, Dogen's rough contemporary, a Pure Land priest named Shinran Shonen, married without hiding the fact nor renouncing his clerical status. He said of himself that he was "neither a monk nor a layperson." Functionally, he was creating a noncelibate priesthood not unlike he Anglican priesthood, as opposed to the celebate Roman Catholic one. Within the Pure Land school, unlike Zen and the other Buddhist denominations, married clergy, neither monks nor laypeople, were openly acknowledged from that time.

Many years later, Suzuki Roshi used that term when speaking of his students as neither monks nor laypeople. However, his meaning was somewhat different from Shinran's. He was describing the emerging Zen practitioners of North America and the West. And he really meant all of them, whether they chose to follow an adaptation of the Japanese ordination model, or, ever more frequently, simply chose to be householder practitioners.

When Zen first began to emerge in medieval China, householder practitioners were few and far between, and as I noted, they were usually only highly educated governmental officials.

Officials with time they could devote to something beyond bare survival. Few were interested in a traditional monastic life as monks or nuns. Later, in Japan, some were interested in Zen priest practice as it evolved there. But the real focus was learning to meditate, being guided in going deep in those disciplines, and to a lesser degree establishing Mahayana Buddhist lives. While at the same time making their livings outside of a professional Buddhist world.

Over the centuries, Zen centers emerged to serve that community. The San Francisco Zen Center is a major complex with three branches: the original in San Francisco, the monastery in Tassajara Hot Springs, and the Green Gulch Farm in Marin County. It serves a network of affiliated communities, at this writing with nearly seventy formal sanghas in North America alone, and many more overseas.

This has become something of a pattern for her Zen centers in the West. There are ordained practitioners. There are monastics. There are Zen priests in the Japanese style. And through a separate evolution, the Korean Taego Order also includes non-celibate clergy; they are beginning to have a significant presence in North America and the West.

Whatever the tradition, many of these practitioners are householders.

Another Korean derived lineage, the Kwan Um School of Zen, originally saw a two-fold leadership rising, monastics and householders. Over the last decades I've watched the numbers of monastics shrink steadily, to the point that today the teachers of their extensive community are nearly entirely householders. Similarly, the linage of the late Chinese master Sheng Yen is beginning to have a presence outside of the Chinese community through its householder teachers.

And householder teachers and non-celibate clergy reflect the profound shift in who identifies as a Zen practitioner in the West.

Those involved in Zen are not congregants, not, as it were, listeners only. They are not passive in their participation. They have regular disciplined spiritual lives. Not exactly monastic. Not precisely lay. They find their practice supported by the centers and smaller sanghas, which often has a leader who may be ordained, but often is not.

Then there's one more term that has changed its meaning. Originally *sangha* was reserved for a community of monks or nuns. In the Mahayana tradition it quickly became a term for the great community of Buddhists, and even for the great community of life, and beyond that to everything that has emerged. So sangha has come to mean those universal things and the community of practioners. Sometimes just a hanful, sometimes a substantial number, gathered together for practice and mutual support.

Today there are many hundreds of Zen centers and sanghas in many different lineages and traditions, where the majority of the community are householders. Many are best described as neither monastics nor laypeople.

A new community of practice and awakening with new institutions to support the practice and practitioners. The emerging Zen sanghas.

RETREATS AND A NOTE ON WHAT TO DO WHEN YOU CAN'T

"If a word is worth a coin, silence is worth two."
(The Talmud)[1]

Retreats are at the core of today's Zen practice. In some ways they're the place where monastic and householder practice come together. Having a sense of what they are, and some of the tensions in our evolving western forms of Zen might be helpful.

As an old Zen hand, I'm reluctant to tell non-Zen friends I'm off to a retreat. When I do, too often the response is something along the line of, "Boy, I could use some downtime myself." Me, too. But that "downtime" is far from a description of a Zen retreat.

Zen arose within a monastic context, and its disciplines follow monastic rhythms with hours a day dedicated to the core practice of zazen and koan. However, within the rhythms of the monastery there are also training periods and periods of intense practice. The longer training periods are based in the rainy season retreats of early Buddhist monasticism and seem to be the rhythm of the historic Buddha and his companions. In China and East Asia these are ninety or hundred-day periods.

There are also shorter periods of intensive meditation practice. In Zen traditions these are usually seven days, five days, or

---
[1] Megillah, 18a https://www.sefaria.org/Megillah.18a.12?lang=bi.

three days. Single-day and half-day retreats are also common, although these are more commonly called *zazenkai* or *zenkai*, "zazen group" or simply "Zen group." These shorter times ranging from half a day to seven days devoted to intensive practice have become a hallmark of a serious practice in North America and the West. And it is hard to see a serious transmission of the discipline without these retreats.

Sesshin is a Japanese Zen term. It literally means "to touch the heart-mind." As near as I can tell, the idea of this intensive retreat outside of the context of regular monastic life arises in Japan. Although such practices have been adapted in Chan and Son communities of practice here. The Kwan Um School of Zen, a Korean-derived Zen lineage, fully embraces the practice, calling these retreats *Yong Maeng Jong Jin*, which roughly translates as "intrepid sitting." One can hear echoes of "touching the heart-mind" in that. And I love the colloquial interpretation of YMJJ, as "leaping like a tiger while sitting."

The retreat schedule offers liturgy and dharma talks. Interviews with teachers. There are ritualized meals. And usually some brief breaks. But the backbone of the practice is seven, eight, or nine hours of meditation in a day. There is also a form of sesshin called, "Zen without toys," where the daily schedule is just sitting, and eating, and some sleeping.

An ongoing Zen practice can be maintained with a daily commitment of an hour or two. Or really even with as little as a half an hour a day. I have seen some profit enormously from the Zen way supported solely by this regular meditation regime. This needs to be said, and repeated. But for most people, in order to dig deep, there need to be regular periods of intensive devotion to the discipline.

As Zen has evolved, the backbone of the practice has proven to be two-fold. A regular daily practice, which may or may not be at a center, temple, or monastery. And retreat. Many serious Zen practitioners aim at twenty-eight days of retreat a year, four week-long sesshin in that year.

There are many serious practitioners who are not monastics or priests of the Japanese inheritance, in Taego order, or seniors within the Kwan Um school, two principal lineages from Korea, for whom retreats, particularly longer ones, are required. These practitioners find that they cannot make that much of a time commitment. Family obligations, work, life. This needs to be noted and looked at. At this time the expectations of those longer ninety- and one hundred-day retreats for people being considered for leadership is being debated within western convert communities.

The critical thing here is that the call to the practice is a call to something demanding. But on the floor or on a chair, people need to find their own way. How can we be honest with ourselves and take on the practice in healthy ways for ourselves and those with whom we make our lives?

And a next question from that is how can someone find an authentic practice with little or no time dedicated to retreat? I feel there are two answers. One, is harsh and true. Without periods of retreat, it is extremely hard to get to the nub, to encourage the doubt and faith necessary to the heart opening that is Zen's promise. At the very least, those five- and seven-day retreats. So, if you can, retreat is a critical aspect of the discipline.

But, what about when one can't? Not simply because it is inconvenient. That isn't good enough. Not attending retreats because its inconvenient is like not sitting because of some odd ache or pain. Life hurts and is boring and has hard moments. And Zen retreats intensify the whole of life in those concentrated moments. Lukewarm practice won't produce fruit. Not enough water, not enough fertilizer. Well, other than the fact the spirit does indeed rest where it will, and awakening happens. There is always that. And it is the truest thing.

There are genuine possibilities for those who cannot meet retreat schedules. There is a place as Zen practitioners for people who cannot do retreats, or only very lightly touch them. They need not wait for some next life where life choices and opportunities are more propitious. We have minor children. That's gigantic and true. Our work doesn't allow anything vaguely resembling retreat—a fact on the ground for many of us. Health reasons, too. There are totally authentic reasons why someone can't do retreats. And at the same time, one can genuinely be pursuing the intimate way.

In those cases, and I've seen it, one finds the depth of the practice in those periods when one can sit. That energy is then thrown into the very matters that prevent a formal retreat. And with that one can find the depth and challenge one needs.

Also, there are other ways than the intensive practice of single-mindedly pursuing the intimate. Outside of Japan, throughout the rest of East Asia, Zen is always paired with the Pure Land. Here the faith part of the practice takes the lead. Simple confidence in the unfolding mystery, and finding how we are not in control, and how there is a merciful hand in all this.

The paths of surrender reveal the doubt in different but authentic ways. Even in Japan, it is not uncommon for older practitioners, including teachers, and those called masters to turn to Pure Land practice. In the West, we're only at the beginning of seeing how this might manifest. As a birthright Christian, and today perhaps best called a Christian-adjacent Zen Buddhist, I find my own practice influenced by the Jesus Prayer. Like a Pure Land Buddhist who calls to Amida, my practice is infused with the Jesus Prayer. I'm not alone. Among those born and raised Jewish, I'm seeing similar patterns emerge drawing on that even more ancient tradition. These are not a turning away from the deep pointing of Zen, but rather allowing it to take the shapes that our hearts recognize.

Householder Zen brings the monastery home. Householder practice is in many ways harder. But that's life, isn't it? That said, the Zen way calls us to a full-hearted commitment. So, one hundred percent being a member of a family. And one hundred percent a person of the way.

Squaring the circle becomes the practice.

Finding how it really is not one, nor is it precisely two becomes the koan.

WAKING UP IN THE KITCHEN

> *Simplicity, simplicity, simplicity! I say, let your affairs be as two or three, and not a hundred or a thousand; instead of a million count half a dozen, and keep your accounts on your thumb nail.*
>
> (Henry David Thoreau)[1]

For Zen to become something other than a strange hobby, we need to find how it becomes our ordinary lives.

I vividly recall a conversation with a handful of friends, none of them Zen people. The conversation turned to spiritual practices. The circles I move in. One friend offered how every year he ironed a shirt as a spiritual practice. He described in detail how he proceeded, and it was a good description of the structure of both ironing a shirt and a spiritual discipline. The problem was that it was ironing a shirt only once a year.

Everyone laughed. He was kidded mercilessly, starting with the big question. What did his wife think of his spiritual practice? Similarly, in my early Zen days women practitioners occasionally ruefully noted that cleaning the Temple toilets was considered a spiritual discipline. All of a sudden, the men were all agog to take on the task. Several women openly mused about how long this would last.

Now my ironing friend was not wrong. He outlined how he prepared for the practice. And he described the full-heartedness

---

[1] Henry D. Thoreau, from *Walden: Or, Life in the Woods*, chapter 2.

of every part of ironing a shirt. And, in Zen we do say one time could do it.

> Those who try zazen even once
> Wipe away beginningless crimes.[2]

We can in a moment see into the heart of the matter. And there's no reason why carefully ironing around buttons one time might in fact do the trick. And usually it does not. For most of us there are tens of thousands of shirts waiting. Although each contains that possibility, where we get it right, and that spirit rests on the iron.

It's important to see how ironing could be a spiritual practice. Could be for any of us. There's the element of discipline, of regularity, of digging deep. These are generally necessary hallmarks of a genuine practice. Doing it over and over again is, for most of us, most of the time, going to also be part of the deal.

Any of the regular activities of our daily lives can become a significant part of our spiritual disciplines. And so, likewise, cleaning and cooking are the stuff of Zen practice.

When I cook, the first step is cleaning up. Preparing to prepare the meal. I find it an invitation into the sacred moment. If I'm working from a recipe, I read it once or twice. I set out the ingredients, spices, etc. Then I try to do just one thing at a time, and not to fret about the rest of the project. I attempt to proceed deliberately, aware of each step, giving it my full attention. I try not to look at the instructions again until I've finished the step. I proceed this way to the end.

In all these practices I've found often that less is more. I suspect this is the underlying principle of the conscious lifestyle

---

[2] Hakuin, Empty Moon Zen Liturgy Book, np, 2023, 7. https://www.emptymoonzen.org/wp-content/uploads/2023/09/EMZ-General-Liturgy-5th-Edition.pdf.

choice of voluntary simplicity, and Thoreau's oft-cited "simplicity, simplicity, simplicity."

The secret sauce, if you will, is all along the way, to pause. And notice. The other ingredient is: Repeat.

One of the great Zen traditions is formal meal practice.[3] Its roots trace to the lives of early Buddhist monastics, where the robes and the begging bowl were the essentials of entering the ordained path. Later in Chinese Zen the "robe and bowl" were the symbols of transmission, recognition of deepest insight. And along the way formal disciplines emerged, rituals of eating. In Japanese and Korean Zen, these would become fairly detailed. With the Koreans more simply, with the Japanese ever more detailed.

While it is possible to get lost in those details, such as how you hold your hands and even how you use your fingers, something powerful is presented. Doors open. I've found during retreat that eating can be among the most transformative moments, constant invitations into a presence filled with attention and gratitude. Equal to or even more powerfully inviting than formal meditation or liturgy.

There are numerous articles on the internet, and videos on YouTube that provide detailed instructions for the monastic or retreat meal. Here I want to offer a simple outline for oryoki-inspired mindful eating. Six steps:

1. Prepare the space. Set out what you will need. There's no need for it to be the formal Zen bowls and cloths. Use your ordinary plates, bowl, a glass or cup, utensils. Arrange then in some manner. I recommend using

---

[3] In Japanese Soto Zen this is called *oryoki*. Oryoki means "just enough." In Rinzai the practice is called for the bowls, *jihatsu*. And in Korean Son, *gongyang*, meaning offering.

our western traditions for table settings, modified to your situation. Google Emily Post, if you need. Arrange the containers with the prepared food.

2. Pause. Set an intention of gratitude. Place your hands in gassho, putting the palms together and your hands lifted to about where the tips of the fingers are parallel to your eyes. Perhaps say a grace. The Japanese often say *Itadakimasu*. In English that is simply, "I gratefully receive this." Or, perhaps something from your childhood. Something that touches your heart. The Zen rituals provide a list of ancestors on the way, which can be either used in whole or in part, as you find useful. Google "oryoki chants." It can be a guide for your own list of those to whom you are grateful for bringing you to this moment. And always, like Meister Eckhart said, if the only prayer we ever say is thank you, it will be enough.

3. Serve the food. Try to be conscious of the act of picking up bowls or other containers. In Zen centers, things are often picked up with both hands as an invitation into doing that one act fully. Appreciate the physicality of serving. Notice.

4. Do it quietly. And with attention. Traditionally this is a communal meal. But of course, you can do it by yourself. If doing this as a spiritual practice, try eating in silence. I recommend eating silently for the first five minutes or so. Then, with

a signal to the group, begin speaking conversationally. When talking, try not to lose sight of the moment, the food, as well as your companions, and all that the moment brings and means.
5. As you move toward the end, pause. Perhaps offer another intention or prayer of gratitude in closing. In formal oryoki, as one moves toward cleaning up, a special offering is made for hungry ghosts—those perhaps mythological beings whose greed has caused them to be reborn with enormous stomachs and tiny mouths, beings who can never get enough, who are never satisfied. Remembering them, and perhaps ourselves within them, is a powerful moment.
6. Clean up. Washing dishes can be a powerful extension of the practice.

The invitation in this, and in all these moments of invitation, is to notice our ordinary and our sacred lives are not two.

SPIRITUAL DIRECTORS AND TEACHERS

> *"Good friends, companions, and associates are the whole of the spiritual life."*
> (The Buddha)[1]

Zen is very much a path of spiritual direction. Human beings guiding other human beings.

The odd ghost might offer a lesson, and there can be no doubt texts ancient and modern are extremely important, but the real teacher has always been flesh and blood. A teacher is someone experienced in the way and almost always formally acknowledged within the tradition. There are natural healers, but personally, in a medical crisis I want someone with a medical degree and a license.

Much of the Zen discipline is finding the right teacher and then settling into a many-years-long relationship.

And.

I've always been fond of those stories of Nasreddin. He's known by several variations on his name, thanks to Idris Shah, he is known most commonly among English speakers as the Mulla Nasrudin. While there's probably a real person who lived through much of the thirteenth century, we know him as a trickster figure. The anecdotes by and about him contain much of Near Eastern folk wisdom.

One I've heard in a couple of versions has him sitting in a tavern with some companions. One says, "Why is it, Nasreddin,

---

[1] Kalyāṇamittasuttta, Samyutta Nikaya 3:18, trans. Bhikkhu Sujato. https://suttacentral.net/sn3.18/en/sujato?lang=en.

that you've never married?" We need to set aside the fact that in most stories he is very much married. But in this story, well, we need the set-up. The mulla sighs deeply and says, "I spent most of my life looking for the perfect woman." "Ah," another of his companions says, "And you never found her." "Oh, no," exclaimed Nasreddin. "I did indeed. She lives just outside of Baghdad." "Then what happened?" Another deep sigh from the mulla. "Sadly, she wanted a perfect man."

These days I'm much taken with the assertion among some evolutionary scientists that evolution is not, and never has been, in pursuit of perfection. It's always about survival and the continuation of the species. But the mechanisms of that are all about being good enough. This doesn't mean mediocrity. That's not really the point. The point is that in life, as in evolution, in our human relationships, the us that is, often turns out to be enough. Good enough is good enough.

I believe we really need spiritual directors on the Zen way. The tradition is built upon the myth of teacher and disciple, of mind-to-mind meeting, and of a mysterious transmission symbolled at one time by the passing on of a robe and a bowl. I've had cause to think about this a lot over the years. I think of my teachers. I think of the teachers I've met. I think of my own work as a spiritual director.

Early in my Zen life, when I was a monastic at Shasta Abbey, a new monk joined our community. The buzz among us was that he was a fully transmitted Obaku priest, which we knew was a sub-branch of the Rinzai schools. As the weeks unfolded, it came out that he had just made up these ordinations.

While he was the first fraudulent teacher I would meet, over the years there have been a number of such individuals. Some I've known personally. Often, they're charming rogues. Sometimes it's shocking that they have any kind of following at all. They leave trails of something unsavory behind them. Some even have something to offer. But each had decided the best route to teaching authority was simply to make up their authorizations. Always there are negative consequences.

Over the years, there have been fewer and fewer of these people who just make it all up. Sadly, I believe, because getting a "real" authorization has become so very easy. I've met and read the teachings of a lot of people who have real enough titles, but who seem to have little insight into the deep matter, much less the tradition itself. These people can only be problematic teachers. Even in a tradition where the student is actually more important than the teacher.

Dharma transmission is both a myth, in all senses of that word, and a historical fact. It arises in early medieval China, which in its Confucian inheritance was deeply concerned with relationships. You need to know where you came from, and who your ancestors were. Out of this, the early uniquely Chinese Buddhist meditation schools began to construct a lineage chart that went back to the Buddha himself.

However, starting with the disciples of Damon Hongren in the seventh century, this mythic chart rapidly became something historic. And for better than a thousand years, Zen has been defined in significant part by its claim of a lineage of Dharma transmission. A "special transmission outside of the scriptures, not founded upon words and letters."

It is often oversold. The rhetoric around it is just so grand.

It often suggests that awakening and its recognition by a teacher is in some way disconnected from our ordinary lives. And that the mastery of transmission means one is no longer bound by the laws of cause and effect. A sad state of affairs when reality happens.

What we need is not a perfect master. What we need is competence, someone who has walked the path longer than we have, has experienced what she has experienced, and is skillful enough to see how it might apply to our own lives. Mine. Yours. We need a good enough teacher way more than some plaster saint.

What dharma transmission really is, when it is being true, is fairly simple. It means that someone who has transmission in the lineage sees in another person three things: a sense of awakening, the ability to guide people in Zen meditation, and the capacity to take on spiritual direction, what in the West is sometimes called the cure of souls.

Depending on the school, the ordering of importance for these three things is different. All expect someone to be able to guide others in the disciplines of Zen meditation. Pretty much everyone understands the need for this skill, and it is often the most obvious reason someone is given transmission. They're good at meditation and they seem capable of guiding others.

Few seem to give a lot of attention to having a sense of usefulness to people in their care over a long period of time. Mostly this is picked up over time by a teacher. This is a good reason for finding a teacher who has been doing it for a while.

Then there's awakening. In the mythic version of transmission this is what it's all about. So. Has someone with transmission seen deeply into the matter of not one and not two? Given our stories, one reasonably should be able to expect this. But in many Zen lineages this is not at all the case. Instead, years of practice, monastic experience, and the ability to lead a retreat are the markers. While it isn't an absolute, for the most part only lineages with an emphasis on traditional koan training expect some sense of awakening to boundlessness, to nonduality.

I was for several years involved in a conversation about minimum standards within the Soto branches of our convert Zen communities. There were three camps. First were those who wished to carry over the training expectations of the Japanese Sotoshu, the institution our priestly credentials all traced to. Second were those who felt there needed to be substantial reforms to address the unique conditions here in the West, and specifically North America. And third were those who felt dharma transmission was all that was required, and training didn't matter.

Each of these approaches have produced good and bad teachers, but the single requirement of dharma transmission has been the weakest link, creating people with credentials with little meaning to them. The "we only need dharma transmission" camp has been the primary source of teachers with extremely limited formation. Such teachers often gravitate to the internet and social media. Their teachings tend to reflect reading, sometimes a lot of it, but not a lot of practice. And often show little evidence of actual encounters with the fundamental matters of the heart. Lots of right and wrong, not a lot of invitation into intimacy. With just enough exceptions to make me draw short of any blanket assertion.

There will always be those more concerned with titles. There will always be snakes with the dragons. Always. All that noted, I believe the backbone of our North American Zen will continue to be those attempting to adapt as closely as possible the patterns we've inherited. This includes expecting monastic experience as central to formation.

However, there is very much a growing edge, seeking rigor in formation, while acknowledging we are no longer primarily a monastic movement. And creating ways to continue finding depth in our paths, without necessitating going into a monastery. We are witnessing some very exciting possibilities for new shapes for Zen among some of these groups.

So, you want a teacher. How do you sort through the people on offer?

Today we have the advantages as well as the problems in access to internet searches. Look for people who are clear about who authorized them. If they don't, you can safely move on. If they have stated their relationships, and you don't know who the listed teachers are, look them up. You should be able to trace the lineage back into traditional charts.

Then what about their formation? What kind of training did they have? And what do other people say about them? Don't let the fact they might be controversial stop you if they otherwise seem like the sort of teacher right for you. Dig a bit deeper. And make your own decisions.

And remember good enough.

Today Zen teachers come through lineages transmitted through China, Japan, Korea, and Vietnam. There are traditional monastics, mostly in Chinese, Korean, or Vietnamese lines. There are non-celibate priestly lines from Japan and Korea. And there are Householder lineages, mostly derived from Japan, but there are Korean and Chinese lines as well. These Householder teachers are becoming increasingly important.

While there are some attempts at creating organizations of Zen teachers, none has universal acceptance, and I can't say that any offers sufficient quality control and oversight. Perhaps the American Zen Teachers Association, which is meant only to be a support group, is of some use. At least in the sense that its membership consists of peoplewho all recognize one another as mutually recognizable as Zen teachers. And as a result of their trying to set parameters defining who fits, they have come up with some rough guidelines. The AZTA considers about three years of retreat, accomplished either through traditional ninety or hundred-day retreats, or in day-long or week-long retreats, as a necessary if not sufficient condition. So we get at least that. At the same time, there are totally qualified and competent teachers who do not belong to the AZTA.

Any Zen organization should have clear ethical guidelines. It means the institution is paying attention to basics. This has followed a range of scandals, mostly of a sexual nature, among the first and second generation of Zen teachers. I wouldn't recommend a group that doesn't have such clear guidelines. But one needs to understand that, in smaller organizations, and organizations that rely heavily on teachers, the guidelines are only as good as the teachers and their senior students make them.

I suggest you consider teachers who followed clear paths to insight, and who clearly state this is their primary project. Usually this means people who've had extensive training on the koan way. But, again, any categorical assertion should be suspect here. The right fit is the right person.

There is sort of a bottom line to this. Seek with an open heart. And open eyes.

Take your time. And then, when the time is right, throw yourself into the project with all your heart.

THE MATTER OF WAKING UP AND GROWING UP

Buddhism was there as I helped my kids brush their teeth. As I drove the carpool, grocery shopped, tied shoes, and wiped noses. As a mother, every moment is an opportunity to practice. Parenting was my spiritual practice, and parenting was indeed a form of Engaged Buddhism.
(Leslie Davis)[1]

One of the things I've noticed about our lives as people of the way, both as individuals and as emerging institutions (for lack of a more accurate term), is that we often miss this: that the spiritual way involves two things going on at the same time.

Waking up. And growing up. They're not the same thing. But if they don't travel together, it's unlikely we'll win the great hope of healing for ourselves or the world.

One of the intriguing things about taking on a spiritual path is that most of the naturally arising negative aspects of our lives will present. Usually from pretty early on. And we have the choice to deal with them or not.

If not, well, our career following the spiritual path will be either extremely slight, or somewhere along the line will just plain end. When we determine to enter the intimate way, almost immediately we start encountering difficulties. Turns

---
[1] Leslie Davis, "Engaged Parenting as Spiritual Practice, *Lion's Roar,* March 2019, https://www.lionsroar.com/engaged-parenting-as-spiritual-practice/.

out we are most of the early difficulties. That is, you. That is, me.

Throughout the ages, people who have walked the intimate way have offered signposts for us. And they've named many of the difficulties. And often, they've ired them with positive attributes that correspond to the negative things. For me, negativity shifted to curiosity, and over the years toward a generally positive disposition in the face of common failings.

Zen upholds a consciousness that is "neither one nor two." That place of awareness neither trapped in the natural dualism of our reasoning function, nor within a pervading sense of unity or boundlessness. This is called by several names, but I tend to prefer "awakening."

That awakening is also tied up with a small cluster of spiritual disciplines. Most are focused on silent meditation, with a tradition of encounter stories which are engaged as invitations into ever deeper perspectives of awakening. That place which is not one, nor two.

These two facets, an awakened heart or mind, and a cluster of disciplines, are not enough to make a stool, a foundation.

But there is a third leg. Beyond that sense of awakening and spiritual practices, there are the precepts. They can be seen as moral imperatives not unlike the Ten Commandments. They are the place where waking up and growing up most obviously meet.

Taken together, these are the three aspects—the three legs of Zen. Awakening and the practices and the precepts. While precepts are common to all schools of Buddhism, within Zen they take on some unique shades of emphasis.

Here I want to limit ourselves to the core five precepts.

In one sense, they're the precepts Gautama Siddhartha gave to laypeople, Householders. They also form the first five precepts of monastic ordination, although the precept concerning sexuality is understood differently by householders and monastics.

In Zen they also come by way of a probably fifth-century Chinese scripture, the *Brahmajala Sutra*, the Brahma Net, which features ten major and forty-eight minor precepts. The first five of the major precepts are nearly identical with the monastic codes. Again, sexuality is understood differently for monastic and householder. Also, the vow concerning intoxication is about dealing in alcohol. But the warning about intoxication is still there.

Whether from the monastic codes or the Chinese tradition, these first five feel and in many ways are straight forward:

1. Do not kill. It's a complicated precept. In one sense it's impossible. We breathe and we kill thousands of microbes. We walk, millions die. I've found this a caution and an invitation. The caution is that no matter what we wish, life is messy. And sometimes terrible. And our own actions are pretty much always complicit. The invitation that comes with this is to find some generosity of heart. Treasure life, and be grateful.

2. Do not steal. There isn't a precept that doesn't have an exception. One of the family stories from my life comes from when my grandmother worked as a live-in maid. She was accused of stealing food. Clearly in the telling the shame turned on powerlessness. But in my life, I found myself thinking, *If I were hungry, and later if my family were hungry, I might hesitate, but if I couldn't find another way, I would steal.* Usually, what we're being called into with this precept is to respect things. To respect the place of things, and to respect that we do not end

at our skins. The things in our lives can be and are often important.

3. Do not misuse sexuality. This one is reinterpreted by every generation. We humans rage about sex, from one pole to another. Libertine and Puritan. Here I find we're called into intimacy. We are invited to honor our own bodies, and treat other's bodies with the same respect.
4. Do not lie. Honesty is not always the best policy. Few are going to be completely truthful all the time. And those people are not liked. And sometimes are dangerous. But the deep calling of telling the truth is a matter of respect, finding our relationships, and living with integrity.
5. And do not use drugs. This is the constant call to clarity. To not be deluded. Again, most of us are deluding ourselves all the time. Is a glass of wine a problem? Maybe yes, probably no. Are there too many hours of watching television? Of course. But how many and under what circumstances? The invitation is to see how we delude ourselves, and create paths of clarity in our personal affairs and in our dealings with others.

There's a Ten Commandment feel to these precepts, especially in that "do not" formulation. But, in fact, they're more complicated. Or, maybe the Ten Commandments are more complicated than one finds in a bare read. Within that complexity many people engage the precepts from an invitational perspective: Foster life. Respect the integrity of things, their boundaries.

Respect your body and other's bodies. Speak truthfully. And live into your clarity of experience and vision.

Of course, that's nowhere near the end of the matter. When we think of them as part of that three-legged stool of the intimate way, of the path of awakened hearts, their significance becomes clearer. Not just good ideas. Not just crowd control. But something more.

One of the gifts of Zen is that physicality, the acknowledgement we are bodies. We don't occupy our bodies for a while; we are our bodies. Zen isn't overly concerned with larger views of post-mortem existences. It has no problem with the larger Buddhist story of cycles of suffering and the dream of release. But this path of awakening can fit into other stories of that sort, as well. Like those of Abrahamic traditions. Because the stories matter less than who we are in this moment. The one that is a body—and how we live with it.

So sometimes the precepts are just rules. There are times in our lives when we just need rules. But they can also be descriptive of what the awakened life looks like. They describe the Bodhisattva heart, and they show the great vow of our going together.

So, what about those times when we just need the rules? Much of our lives we're wandering around in the thickets. Without a clue. We're lost. And the precepts can become a lifeline thrown out to us. Sometimes we just have to grab that line.

Contrary to the solipsistic misunderstanding of Zen Buddhism promulgated here and there, particularly on the web, Zen is not an anarchist's spiritual dream. One of the first things we find as we begin investigating ourselves and our place in this world, is that we do not exist alone. It is not all about me. Never has been. And to live as if it's all about me is to invite terrible consequences. Here is an inescapable truth: everything we do has consequences. Oftentimes, in our headlong rush of living, we need some external guidelines, a trustworthy set of rules by which to mark what we're up to.

But if we live only in the realm of rules, we are strangled by dead letters. And not only are our own lives constrained, we become caricatures of our true potentiality.

We also need to recall how we are so profoundly tied up together, how our individual lives are each completely woven out of each other. We are more intimate than the words can ever convey. We are all relatives. We're all family. The precepts tell us, do not kill, do not steal, do not lie, don't misuse your sexuality, and don't become intoxicated. We can encounter these words in ways that become the living expressions of this intimate dance of life.

Here the precepts open to a way of life that is creative, expressive, and inviting. And, as they say on late night television, wait, there's more.

Each moment of our lives, as we face death, as we open our mouths to speak, as we encounter each "other" in our lives, as we seek intimate moments with another, each of these events turns out to be a gate. And if we get it, if we notice the gate, what was once a barrier is thrown open, and we find our way through to a boundless freedom.

That's where we find the deepest invitation of precept as koan. Unfortunately this one needs to rest as an assertion and as an invitation…

But it is there, Guanyin's mercy, the universe itself lurking in the shadows of our actions and thoughts, a divine mugger just waiting for you to walk into the dark places…

Try it. You might not like it, but you'll be grateful…

PART FOUR
DIRECT POINTING

The most distinctive feature of Zen's spiritual disciplines is koan introspection. Part of the value of koans, in addition to a direct presentation, is the invitation. Here we can find invitations not only into the deeper matter of that saying, *I am not it, but in truth it is me.* This includes the intimate dance of insight. But it also includes the possibilities of application throughout the course of our lives. We find that wider aspect mostly in comments on texts.

A KOAN ABOUT TOILET PAPER

A student of the way asked Yunmen, "What is Buddha?" Yunmen replied, "Dried shit stick."
(Gateless Gate)[1]

Yunmen is one of the great teachers of the Zen way. He was born in the middle of the ninth century and died late in the middle of the tenth century. The story of his awakening is one of the classics.

After traveling from teacher to teacher, following hints and suggestions, he came to master Bokushu's solitary hut. He was met by the master himself, who opened the door, looked at the student, and shut the door in his face. Yunmen knocked a second time, the master opened the door, looked at him again, and shut the door in his face again. Yunmen knocked again. This time when the master opened the door, he set his foot in the door jam. Bokushu looked down, looked up and said, "Speak!" Yunmen hesitated and the master slammed the door shut, breaking Yunmen's foot.

And in that moment when his foot broke, Yunmen saw into the fundamental matter. He would carry the mark of this encounter for the rest of life as a severe limp.

Yunmen would become one of the great teachers of his time, with more than sixty Dharma successors. His line would

---
[1] Gateless Gate, Case 21, author's version.

eventually become one of the tributaries of the Linji line, the Rinzai school in Japan.

As a teacher he was often just as direct as Bokushu. And often to great effect.

For instance, that dried shit stick is a response to one of the great setups of the Zen koan tradition. In the Gateless Gate that question, "Who or what is Buddha?" is asked and answered, if I recall correctly, four times. One of these answers is "three pounds of flax," while another is "this very mind is Buddha." Digging into how these different responses are each correct is part of the path of discernment.

Of those two, one response may seem a complete non sequitur, while the other feels too philosophical for a Zen koan answer. That is, koans are always invitations into intimacy, and their primary purposes are never philosophical.

Then there's the "shit stick" response. This response, this answer, particularly for anyone used to reading spiritual literature, can be unsettling. The scatological response is so unspiritual. At least generally outside Zen circles.

I've seen Zen teachers play up that unsettling quality with considerable gusto. I once attended a talk given by the Korean Zen master Seung Sahn, who addressed this koan. His accent was heavy. In order to make sure his audience understood what he was saying, he leaned slightly to one side and pointed toward his bottom, saying "Shit, shit…" As I recall over the many years between that moment and as I write this, he smiled slightly as he pointed and repeated "shit." A small smile, almost a smirk.

Shit. Shit stick as in a corncob, shit stick as in toilet paper.

What is Buddha? What is the deepest truth? Toilet paper.

I've seen some commentators assert that the shit stick has no intrinsic meaning. The intent is, in fact, to shock. I don't really think so. The playing it up, the leaning over and pointing at one's butt, is playfully drawing us toward something. And it is not a non sequitur. It is not about meaninglessness. Nor is it iconoclasm, a deliberate mocking of spiritual conventions. No more so than three pounds of flax, and no less so than this very mind is Buddha.

The point lies elsewhere.

In some ways this response is a bit like Mu.

Mu is one of the great koans. It is the one many people first encounter when taking up koan practice with a spiritual director within the tradition.

A student of the way goes to the master Zhaozhou, and asks, "Does a dog have Buddha nature?" It's sort of an inside joke question. The standard teaching of the Mahayana way, of Zen, is that everything has, or more properly is, Buddha nature. There are, no doubt, shades of questions within that question as the student presents her question. It feels like it burns within her. And meeting that, Zhaozhou responds, "No." Generations of students have taken up that no, and what it might point to.

A brief word or phrase where the meaning of that word has been vacated, and the sound, the noise itself is the presentation. It is also an invitation. A principle of koan engagement is assuming a direct pointing, and with that, we discover for ourselves an invitation into intimacy. And often that pointing and that invitation come from what seems to be left field.

In fact, this story gives us a direct meeting of the question. And we need to start with the question. People come in every condition. Sometimes our questions are showing off what we know, or think we know. Sometimes our questions are buying time until we get the lay of the land. Sometimes we haven't a clue, and our questions are the real non sequiturs. And sometimes, we are ripe, and our questions are burning. Our bodies are the burning question, trying to touch the real matter.

I'm very taken with that. Shit. Night soil. Fat white maggots. And that steaming, fecund Buddhahood.

While the primary pointing is, well, to the primary point, we can also catch other hints of possibility, of the richness that is this way. All of it, all of our lives are the stuff of our awakening. Even our shit. All the different kinds of shit. Our brokenness, our failures, our addictions.

All of it, steaming with Buddhahood. And that takes us back to the primary point. The ingredients of our lives are also the ingredients of our awakening. Toilet paper. Corncob. Shit stick.

Just this.

A KOAN ABOUT WHAT IS ALIVE

The master of the intimate way Yuean Shanguo said to a student of the way, "Xizhong, who invented the wheel, made a hundred carts." Then the master asked, "If you take off the wheels, the axle, and the rest of it, what would be vividly apparent?"

(Gateless Gate)[1]

Yuean Shanguo was a teacher in the Linji linage at the beginning of the twelfth century. He was a dharma ancestor of Wumen, who compiled the Gateless Gate. As with some of the best teachers, we know almost nothing about him. Not where he was born, not where he died.

In Chinese mythology, Xizhong invented both the wheel and the cart. Our western Zen ancestor Robert Aitken Roshi notes the implied play where the same ideogram is used for wheel and cart. It's similar to English where a car can be known by the slang term "wheels." A Zen practitioner's imagination can be sparked by wheels. The wheel of the dharma might come to mind. And in Zen that still space at the middle of all the motion might generate a mind bubble, or two.

Of course, the case is about removing the wheels. Removing the axle. Removing the buckboard. The seat. Tossing away the

---
[1] Gateless Gate, Case 8, author's version.

whip. All of it. And with that, the question: What about then? Now? In the moment, this moment. What shines forth?

What we're invited into here is a place beyond our ideas of what is, and of what is not. We're welcomed to the other side of our ideas. That place before we put words to it. Finding that place is critical to a full life. It is an invitation into the world of not one, not two. We need to see through our fictions about the world and ourselves. However we aren't meant to live in that place. We need the world of form and things.

When we find both, then things happen.

I think about the religious perspectives of hunter-gatherer cultures. It's one of the things people look at when hoping to get a glimpse of what people thought of as sacred matters before religions got organized. It's a necessarily flawed process. But it's what we've got.

With various cautions, what we see when we look at hunter-gatherer cultures is animism. The nineteenth-century anthropologist Edward Tylor coined the term "animism," drawing on the Latin for breath. It addresses a perspective that seems to arise in pre-agricultural cultures around the world. I like how breath, spiritual, once again visits us.

Now, we need at the same time to be aware that when looking at these cultures, we're not actually looking at the dawn of religions. What we see, looking at hunter-gatherers, are things happening now, marked with the same weight of the many thousands of years that we're all heirs to. That said, while it is through a glass darkly, it's what we have.

And what they have is animism. The first observation was that in these cultures everything is animated, everything possesses a spirit or is spirit itself. That continues. But what it means, well, that's been a bit more slippery.

At the beginning, Professor Tylor, actually the very first professor of anthropology at Oxford, thought animism was a confusion of categories. It seemed a collapsing of animals and plants and inanimate things. And within that, seeing them all joined by *anima*, as noted, literally "spirit." He thought it was a mistaken view common to early humans. But he also felt it the building block of all religions to come.

The good professor's view about evolution, and distinctions between primitive and advanced, are no longer held by, well, by most any serious academics looking at the matter. His tracking of a path to monotheism is seen as a kind of triumphalism that doesn't stand up to close examination.

But there is a reclaiming today of animism. And I find this is important. Animism is now better understood as seeing that the universe is composed of persons, only some of whom are human. This calls us to notice things, and to notice how we know that we are in relationship with all other things. It is a powerful call to intimacy.

So, animism is an approach to life that is based in relationships. It is a world filled with subjects rather than objects. Everything is relational. I've been quite caught by that idea of a relational epistemology. Particularly how that fits within the Zen tradition, which calls us to notice the worlds of form and emptiness. And for us right now, how it touches Xizhong and his magical cart.

First there's that world of form. In our human minds we usually get the "form" thing. It's where we live. In the koan, of course, it's the cart. We can touch it. Perhaps we can smell it. All our senses can engage it. And we can tell stories about carts.

But then there's that empty thing. What exactly is that? For us on the Zen way it's the first nut to crack. Much of our practice is inviting us into an investigation of emptiness, or, as I generally prefer to call it, boundlessness. It's elusive. Noticing it doesn't come naturally. After all, it seems a complete contradiction to the very idea of things. It seems to be a thing without thingness.

Here those two kinds of animism help me. The one is the idea that everything has a spirit. But there's also our being involved in spirit. In fact, in some traditions, like Vedanta, this becomes a oneness. It is atman, a pantheistic God. We find this in some Jewish texts and as a minority report in both Christianity and Islam. It is completely personal. I can't disdain this intimate approach. Where everything is sacred. It is how we humans meet the world when we let go of our ideas of being the apex of creation, the end of a long line of evolution.

It seems that as we come to this particular mystery of our lives, we engage it from places deeper within our hearts than our brains can quite grasp. As in the political constructs of liberal and conservative, to some degree we engage our politics based upon imperatives that are embedded in a place before words arise. Similarly, we seem to engage this greatest of mysteries about who we are in personal and impersonal ways.

And it's hard to judge. It's certainly hard to claim one is right and the other wrong.

But the Zen dharma makes us particularly aware of the traps of projecting our own awareness on this place, this moment, this experience, as a thing, or in any way like a human. It is especially dangerous to paint our own face on that place on the other side of our separating this from that.

Within the Zen way we invite an encounter to a place without categories, or divisions, or a sense even of subjective relationships. At least in the moment of encountering the boundless.

In our tradition we call it not knowing. It is an emptying of categories. Remove the wheels. Remove the axle. Take every nail and plank away.

Now, in the form and emptiness equation, emptiness is form. *That is there* is form. Form is real. To call it illusion is a mistake. Although it is as illusory as a mirror's reflection. To call it a dream is missing the point—although it is a dream. And this contradictory mess has to be dealt with.

So what does that look like when the rubber hits the road?

In my adult life I've always had to struggle with my weight. I can recall during one period when I was lighter, I was talking with someone about the spiritual path and how, if at all possible, one should have a human guide on the way. The person I was speaking with was not a Buddhist or a Zen practitioner. So I recommended someone I knew in his tradition that I admired. He replied, "She's fat. There's no way she can really be spiritual."

The Christian founder Paul the Apostle writes of a thorn in his side, and how it is a constant goad. He never said what it is. Many people have speculated. Some modern theologians have suggested perhaps homosexuality. And there are other theories. The truth for us is that pretty much all of us have those things that don't quite work. Not unlike that famous Ox and its tail.

If you don't know the case, it's pretty simple. There is an Ox. It has passed through the window. All of it. The head and horns, the shoulders. The flanks. Everything but the tail. The question then, is what about that tail? Like this koan of the cart, it is asking us about the relationship between form and emptiness.

Or, to be precise our personal, intimate, most intimate encounter with form and emptiness. Yours. Mine.

We get too far from ourselves, and that tail wags at us. For me today it's trousers that are a bit too tight. That tail. That thorn. That cart.

Here's the secret. The axle. The wheel. Those nails and boards, all are nothing other than the boundless.

You don't have to fix anything before you can realize it. The nails can be rusty. The boards can be old and splintering. Within this world of form, we are a play of causes and conditions. And each cause, each condition is wildly open. Boundless. Empty.

Following the Zen way, I've genuinely had shifts and insights that have helped me see past the two worlds. It's all even integrated into much of my life. And I continue to deal with the issues of my own karma body, only slightly assisted by those insights. There is an interplay of form and emptiness, but there is no transformation into something different. We are what we are and it is boundless. Every bit of it. Thorn. Tail. Cart.

Meeting the cart and knowing it is boundless and that it is a cart. Knowing our particular thorn is boundless and yet it is a thorn. Knowing the Ox on both sides of that window.

Well, with that everything in our lives becomes clear.

So. All that said. It becomes your turn. At that moment, at this moment, what is vividly apparent?

A KOAN ABOUT ZEN TEACHERS

Huangbo said to his assembly "You are all slurping up brewer's dregs. If you're always wandering about, how will you find this moment? Don't you know that in all of China there is not a single Zen teacher? One of the assembly stepped forward and protested. "Bu, there are people all over the country who lead communities and guide practitioners. What about them?" Huangbo responded, "I didn't say there is no Zen, only there are no teachers."

(Blue Cliff Record)[1]

I recall a conversation with someone who asserted there were no Zen masters in North America. He was someone who had studied for some years in Japan. And what he really meant was there were no officially recognized Zen masters in the Rinzai tradition in North America. Although it did sort of feel like he was also implying no "real" teachers of Zen, either. He was wrong on both counts.

Now to be an official Zen master in the Rinzai school in Japan includes a lifetime residence within a Zen cloister. So, these are people devoted to the great project through a single-minded practice, forsaking everything else. And there are maybe thirty

---

[1] Blue Cliff Record, Case 11, author's version.

people in Japan, probably fewer, who are recognized institutionally as Rinzai Zen masters, Shike or Roshi.

Actually, this is true within the Soto school as well. There are no more than about fifty Soto priests holding a version of the Shike rank. And there has never been a North American to hold this rank. One American, Roshi Patricia Dai-En Bennage, was a jun shiki, the rank immediately below. And she was the only one.

This set me to thinking about various things. First, how it's true, we in the West have few Zen masters of that institutional rank. There are in fact a couple of Japanese Rinzai masters, one I can think of who lives here, and a couple of others who visit. And, here is a truth: they bring a quality of presence that is unique. There is something wondrous to be found within a lifetime commitment to that single thing.

There are other people legitimately given the title roshi, both in reformed Rinzai lineages and in the koan-informed Soto reform Harada-Yasutani line. Their training may not involve the lifetime in a cloister, but is very, very rigorous. There are also Soto teachers who don't use koans, but are obviously deeply wise and worthy teachers here.

And then, there's a so what?

I feel there need to be expectations and requirements for someone who wishes to represent the Zen way as a teacher. Otherwise, I just don't see how they can use the word Zen for what they teach in any honest way.

But a teacher who simply meets institutional requirements is what I would call a journeyman. This is a genuine practitioner of the way. But, mastery, well, that's something beyond the ability of any institution to designate, except in the most nominal sense. And I say that with genuine respect for those many shike of both Japanese Rinzai and Soto traditions.

Here the cloister is no longer assumed. And, in fact, nearly impossible to live. The few cloisters that exist here are precarious institutions, and none that I can think of can in fact guarantee a lifetime home. So, nearly everyone has to assume at most a period of retreat, a weekend, a few months, a few years, and then eventually back into the world. One way or another.

And I can't say this is a bad thing. The practice isn't to crush us, but to see through the mystery, to learn to live with the dual truths of form and emptiness. Of course, the deal, the bottom line, is seeing through.

I recall seeing a sculpture on social media. From the side it was a large human head. But straight on it was just slices of metal, almost invisible. And that's almost it. From one angle the mess of the world, from the other, emptiness. But, not quite like the sculpture, in this case both are exactly the same. Although those words don't quite do it either.

Form and emptiness. Not one. Not two.

I have also lived long enough into the Zen way to see several forms of expression that look authentic, that seem to have transformed lives. Individuals who train in these various ways are emerging first and foremost as mature practitioners of the ancient and present way. And some among them are becoming wise counselors.

And, as has always been the case, there are rogues and mountebanks. The robe can hide a multitude of sins. So, caveat emptor. And in between rogue and sage, are many, many people with titles but uncertain skills.

And. And. Among that great cloud of witnesses to our way are some who may deserve the title of master. Rich and complicated times, these. That said, back to the koan.

> Huangbo said to his assembly, "You are all slurping up brewer's dregs. If you're always wandering about, how will you find this moment? Don't you know that in all of China there is

not a single Zen teacher? One of the assembly stepped forward and protested. "But there are people all over the country who lead communities and guide practitioners. What about them?" Huangbo responded, "I didn't say there is no Zen, only there are no teachers."

Huangbo Xiyun is another of the great teachers from the mythic origins of the Zen way during the Tang dynasty. It's uncertain when he was born, but he died in 850. He was a successor to the Baizhang Huaihai, while his most renowned successor was Linji Yixuan, who is considered the founder of the Linji, or in Japanese, the Rinzai school.

Beyond being enormously tall, very little more is known about him. The collection of his teachings, the *Ch'uan-hsin Fa-yao*, unlike most other traditional collections, contains no biographical details beyond those that we can infer from the recorded dharma encounters.

What we have are his teachings. And, well, his successors, particularly as they flow through and become Rinzai Zen. And this case is a delicious example of Huangbo's teachings.

So, here he is berating an assembly of monastics. In those days, they traditionally would wander from monastery to monastery between the formal training periods, meeting masters of the way, encountering peers. And, of course that occasional tea lady who might shake the foundations. He was reminding them of a hard truth. Ultimately, we must turn that light inward.

And seeing through. Seeing both sides of the sculpture. Realizing they are the same thing. Exactly the same thing. And not exactly. Not one. Not two. And the proof of the pudding is how you meet someone in the grocery store.

When we talk about masters and teachers and all of that, like the leading paragraphs of this little reflection, we might forget

A KOAN ABOUT ZEN TEACHERS

what it's all about. And, with that some of the basic promises of the way. One is that we all have what it takes. We need only to stop, to sit down, to shut up, and to notice. Then the ten thousand things stop being our projections, and instead become the very truth of our lives.

Good old Huangbo calls us to that. "Don't you realize in all of the Americas there isn't a single Zen master?" Could he be telling us about institutional titles? Could he be telling us about the quality of North or South American Zen, or maybe European Zen? Or could the invitation be somewhere else?

So long as we have self and other, so long as there is a master and a student, so long as the heart is divided, what do we have?

We're all at the edge of falling into awakening. Every moment, with every breath. In ancient China. In medieval Japan. In our contemporary California. Time flows. Time dances. Then. Now. Future. Let go of it all. Just for a moment. Don't worry, it will return.

But, in this moment, can you find that place where there is no master, there is no teacher? And, of course, no student?

Huangbo slaps his stick in his hand. He glowers, all seven feet of him. Is this the moment?

A KOAN ABOUT A STONE CRYPT

You find yourself in a stone crypt. There are no windows. The sole door is locked from the outside. How are you free?
(Miscellaneous Koans)[1]

Once one realizes that Zen is not about controlling our blood pressure or even capturing a moment of calm in the midst of the gathered storm, we begin to find we are on a pilgrimage. We are on a sacred journey to heal the great hurt, ours and not just ours. To find the meaning of our lives and our deaths, the way to live fully into the wonder, and too often, the horror of it all.

There is a cirriculum based upon the teachings of the eighteenth-century Japanese master Hakuin Ekaku, and there's a program in my lineage. First, one digs deeply into the first koan, what is sometimes called the breakthrough koan; most commonly it's the Mu or dog koan. It's the one that helps us see past the snares of our egos and into the larger mystery. Then we begin to wander through that land, perhaps before only visited in our dreams.

We do this first through a consideration of the Miscellaneous Koans. Later we explore some of the great collections like the Gateless Gate, the Blue Cliff Record, and the Book of Equanimity. The Miscellaneous Koans are specific to the Harada-Yasutani lineage; each lineage offers a slightly different collection. They're curated to meet the needs of a particular time and place.

---

[1] Empty Moon Zen Miscellaneous koans, Case 6, author's version.

A KOAN ABOUT A STONE CRYPT

Here, early on in those Miscellaneous Koans, we find this question:

> You find yourself in a stone crypt. There are no windows. The sole door is locked from the outside. How are you free?

Koans bring a point with them. The poke in the eye. The cold slap from the universe. A call to our hearts. In the face of that, all that: How are you free?

These are strange times. Freakish weather that may no longer be freakish. Politics and crime touching a tad too closely for a republic that relies on some basic trust. A time when mass shootings have slipped off the front page. A time where increasing numbers of women and men are living on American streets. I'm sure you have your own version of the litany.

At first it was sort of casual, just a recollection mentioned by a friend. "Do you remember the stone crypt koan?" But as time has passed the references to this koan have come more frequently and become more visceral.

More and more I feel like I'm in that stone crypt. It's cold. It's dark. I'm beginning to feel afraid. Or at least some disequilibrium.

Mostly we get the idea behind the image of a crypt. At least the intellectual part. No matter who we are, our lives are constrained. We have a lot less control than we want. Whatever our desire for autonomy might be, we always, always will find walls. But then there is constrained and there is constrained. For most people in the affluent West, what increasingly is called the global north, if you're not an hourly worker, you might not even see the walls most of the time. The sense is latent, it arises in our dreams, or maybe in one compulsive behavior or another.

But. Now. Here. In the gathering years since that dreadful plague that swept the globe, many of us who maybe have avoided the harshness of the question, of what that stone tomb genuinely points to, are now finding it right in our faces. And, well, it can be pretty ugly. We're not just in the crypt. The crypt, the tomb is our bodies. It is our minds. It is the stories we tell about ourselves. And.

A lot of people who don't work with koans think they're non sequiturs, words empty of meaning. People who don't practice with them as a spiritual discipline easily confuse them with other word games, as a social media friend recently did with me, citing the question about a tree falling in the woods, and whether there's a sound. Assuming that was a koan.

Word game, maybe. But the stakes are much higher. They speak to who we really are. And, they offer us an invitation to find what that real might be. It is in that context I find myself thinking of Herschel Schacter.

He was a leader of the Modern Orthodox Jewish movement, who died in 2013. But outside of that spiritual community he is mostly recalled for an incident at the close of the Second World War. It was the 11th of April, 1945. Hard to get more specific. He was a Jewish chaplain attached to the VIII Corps of the Third Army that drove into the heart of Nazi Germany.

Because he was with that Corps, Herschel Schacter was the first Jewish chaplain to enter Buchenwald, no more than an hour after its liberation. He witnessed those horrific moments. Smoke rising. The smell of burned bodies. And more corpses everywhere, and living people barely discernable from the dead.

I understand, in a safely distant way, the stench of the camps. It was something horrendous. Walking into Buchenwald was walking into the wreck of a slaughterhouse. It seemed everyone had been murdered, and asked if any Jews were still alive.

He was taken to the barracks, where people too weak to move lay in bunks, confused and terrified, not knowing what was happening. It fell to him to tell them. "*Shalom Aleichem, Yidden,*" he called out in Yiddish. "*Ihr zint frei!*" Peace be upon you, Jews. You are free! He ran to every one of the barracks repeating his call of rescue, of freedom.

The rabbi spent months there, helping. Among the survivors were a thousand orphans, alone and needing tending. Among them was a teenager named Elie Wiesel. I am hesitant to tell such a story here. I don't want to minimize the reality of Buchenwald. We are talking a horror. But what we're invited into is something that is of a piece with this terrible story.

We are being invited into a moment where stars die. And it is hard to look.

It is easy to turn away. I've read that today about a third of Americans don't actually believe there was a Holocaust. More minimize it. Two thirds of millennials don't even recognize the word Auschwitz. So, there we are as human beings. Horrors too terrible to hold. So. We forget. We deny. It's a trick we like to play with reality.

Some things are sufficiently terrible that we don't want to believe them. We certainly don't want to face them squarely.

Sometimes we opt for denial. It's a common human behavior. I believe it is a survival mechanism deep in our consciousness. And denial works. Until it doesn't. And deeper truths await those who don't turn away, don't fall into the slumber of denial. Zen is a way for those who pause and look.

The story that we, each of us, calls "me" is a construct. It is based in real things like genes and experiences. But how it comes together is, well, a stone crypt.

And that's what the koan calls us to. After all our coping devices have failed us. They will. Ultimately, they will. We are all of us mortal. We are all of us constrained. We can deny and limp along. Or we can move in another direction.

So. Then. Now. Here we are. In all our various ways. With our internal worlds and the external world. Each bumping into the other. After all, they're not unconnected. Here where we're living and breathing right now. A lot of people are on the streets. Each damaged in their own way. Mental illness and addiction. Missing two paychecks. Others are not quite there but are in danger of losing their homes. Some are hungry. While some are growing fat within their isolation. Each a blending of harsh realities and dreams of meaning. Real rubber meeting the road time.

With that there is that dreaming world, the interior world. Inside and out are not one. But neither are they two. Here we find mysterious reality. Us. You. And me. A crypt. A tomb. In that moment. In this moment. How are you free?

This is the promise. Once our hearts have opened, just a little, where we get a taste of the reality that the inner and outer worlds are in fact connected. Or, when we notice perhaps more correctly, they're not one, but neither are they two. The connections are subtle. Except when they hit you like a brick. Or a hurricane.

And here you are. Here I am. In a stone crypt. A tomb. Refugees fleeing horrors in Central America. Sitting in a camp in Gaza. Looking for clean water in Flint or Pensacola. The list is very long. And not all of it dramatic. Isolation. Despair. Addiction. In the big scheme, maybe small things. Personal tragedies.

And of course, love, and work that satisfies, and friends. Joys. They all are the tomb.

Can you see the connections? After the stories we tell about them are exhausted, can you notice? After we've set down judgment? And justification? What is then plain as the nose on your face?

I think of Brother Lawrence. He was a peasant in seventeenth century France. He had been a soldier and fought in the Thirty Years' War. He'd been wounded and was lame for the rest of his life. He also had some sort of experience in those horrific times. Some mysterious encounter that would not leave his heart and informed how he acted.

A KOAN ABOUT A STONE CRYPT

After a period of convalescence, he worked as a footman for a nobleman, wearing livery, opening doors, and attending at meals. But this deep encounter that would not leave his heart called him on. Eventually he was admitted as a lay brother in a Carmelite monastery. As a peasant he was not admitted into full vows as a monk and didn't join the monastic choir in the rhythms of monastic prayer. Instead, he worked in the kitchen. He did this for the rest of his life, except toward the end, when his wounded leg ulcerated and he was put to work mending sandals, so he could sit.

We only know about him because people began talking about him. At first simply the other lay brothers, and then peasants who heard about him. He had some sense of grace, something truly and deeply alive just in who he was, that captured people's attention. He was them, totally one of them. And there was something else.

People would meet him and found themselves spilling the wounds of their souls out to him. In response he would give them his attention and, it felt, his love for them just as they were. He wasn't a priest; he couldn't forgive sins. Apparently, he could do something more than that.

Gradually the monks became aware of him. And eventually important people would find their way to the kitchen to talk. One of those important people, a priest named Joseph de Beaufort, collected notes from his visits. After Brother Lawrence died, Beaufort published a small volume about his encounters with this remarkable peasant lay brother.

All that a bit of a long way around to offer some words about the key, not the key to attitude adjustment, to lowering blood pressure, but to something rather more. To something that justifies referencing Buchenwald. To remind people there was such a hell as Auschwitz.

Brother Lawrence wrote of abandoning all specific forms of practice. Instead, he took up a discipline of presence, of attention. He called it a secret conversation with God.

Noticing. All of it. Attending. All of it. Excepting no part. Here in this place, in this body, as this body, as this place. Peace be upon you. You are free.

With that, the invitation. Today, here, now. How are you free?

In this moment, with all the strife and hurt of this world, our shortcomings as human beings, our collaboration with the killers, our fears, our heroic acts, our shameful acts, mostly our small acts—we're involved in all of it: in this moment, how are we free?

The question, which contains the answer. Peace be upon you.

A KOAN ABOUT A BUNCH OF BODHISATTVAS TAKING A BATH

Once upon a time there were sixteen bodhisattvas. It was bath day and they entered the waters together. Simultaneously they all realized the cause of water. They called out as one voice, "This marvelous touch has illuminated all things. We have reached that place where the daughters and sons of the Buddha all dwell!"
(Blue Cliff Record)[1]

I've long loved this case, as we call individual examples of the traditional collected koans. It is also one that my koan teacher John Tarrant was particularly fond of returning to from time to time.

A koan is a matter to be made clear, as the great Zen teacher Robert Aitken told us. Or one may consider a koan as a pointer to some aspect of the great matter of life and death, presented together with an invitation to stand in that place.

A koan is nothing less than an invitation into the healing of our broken hearts.

Their parentage can be varied, ranging from conversations between teachers and students, between teachers, bits of folklore, snippets of poetry. Basically, anything that the teachers of Zen

---

[1] Blue Cliff Record, Case 78, author's version.

find useful. The source of this particular koan can be found in the *Suramgama Sutra*, one of those fascinating Chinese spiritual texts of uncertain provenance.

I'm very much taken with bodhisattvas. Bodhisattvas in our received tradition are people who've seen into the great matter that binds life and death, but who resist passing into the great empty beyond all ideas of separation. That is, until the whole of our suffering world can pass over together.

That little bit of clinging, of resistance brings its own power.

This resistance, this hesitation, this turning back and calling to the many hurting beings, is also a bit of an inside joke for Zen folk. It turns on the fact that we, all of us, every blessed one of us, from you and me, to stars and to elephants, to strands of the Ebola virus, are awakened from before the moment of the explosion of the stars and planets into existence.

We only lack insight into who and what we really are from the ages before our birth. Without that insight we are awash in hurt. So, noticing this truth about who and what we are is a critical thing. Giving our attention to that little bit of frisson, that hesitation, that turning back to the many suffering beings, is the very thing that liberates us all. It is the great turning of our hearts.

That loving glance, the desire to be of use, that surrendering our own liberation for another, is more precious than any marker of wealth. It is the work of the Bodhisattva. It is our work.

Bodhisattvas are the reality of our lives lived authentically. They are what we are at our best, what we are when we surrender our ideas of self and other. A bodhisattva is what we were from before the dancing procession of planets, stars, galaxies, black holes, all of the wonderment of our emergent reality.

And in this case, with this koan we're presented with one of the countless gates into our noticing of that which has always been so. In this case through touch. The touch of water, specifically. But it can be any kind of touch. A lover's touch. A mother's touch. Someone anxious about a friend, her touch. Simply picking up a glass of water. That touch.

And there are those other gates we heard of in the original source of this koan, where awakening is found in each of the different senses. Of course there are numerous gates. In the Zen tradition we name six in particular.

Touch, for one. Here, the touch of water. But also, it could be smell, maybe the smell of that meal your mother prepared revisited tonight. Maybe it's the sound of a crow scolding you as you pass by on an evening walk. Or, possibly, the taste of a perfectly prepared spaghetti dinner.

I recall an evening when Jan and I stood out in front of our condo building looking up into the evening sky and witnessing what they call the blood moon, an amazing total lunar eclipse. I've also noticed that possibility out of the corner of my eye while walking down the street. An unexpected vision, opening the door, inviting my walking through.

I would add that in our Buddhist way, we count six senses. First the five common to us all within our Western inheritance. And. The presentations of our minds as the sixth. The human mind in its amazement, noticing, slicing, dicing, reflecting, predicting. That thing, too.

Gates. Doors. Endless possibilities…

But, also, as my friend, the old Zen hand Stephen Slottow noted, it's important to notice the sixteen bodhisattvas. Not one. Not just you or me. The whole blessed crowd. In fact, we don't realize the deep truths of reality by ourselves. Or, perhaps more correctly, we notice by ourselves, but what we find is that we're all in this mess, wonderful, sad, mysterious, together. Together. Many beings. One body.

Just as it is.

Just as we are.

PART FIVE
FINDING OUR WAY AT THE END OF RELIGION

The world is in chaos. Meaning and direction are hard to find. And Zen, while shaken by the turmoil of the times, has distilled. It has come to offer ways, both traditional and innovative. What are those insights? How do they meet the times? How can Zen help us on our way, in this here, and this now?

ZEN AS MAGICAL REALISM

> *Once upon a time Yangshan Huiji had a dream. In it he traveled to Maitreya's great hall, where he was led up to the third seat. As soon as he sat down a senior monk struck the bell and announced, "Today the one sitting in the third seat will preach." Yangshan immediately stood up, himself gave the bell a strike, and then said, "The truth of the great way is beyond the four propositions and transcends the hundred negations. Listen. Listen."*
>
> (Gateless Gate)[1]

So, putting this whole awakening thing together.

That thing about religion, at least a very big part of it, being about crowd control? Here's the deal. It is true. It's also true of Zen Buddhism. You dig around in any religion that's been here for a while, and it turns out that a big part of its framework is devoted to that social cohesion thing. It's a critical aspect of a culture. Religion reinforces obedience to the king or the republic or whatever stands as the center of the culture.

More sympathetically presented, and also true, this aspect of religion is about the glue to community. It is traditionally where the symbols and rites that tie people together happen. We can see this among oppressed people, who find their religion is the thing

---
[1] Gateless Gate, Case 25, author's version.

that stands between them as a people and oblivion.

Buddhism, when it came to China, needed to show the emperor and court that it was useful to the state. If it hadn't, there would be no Chinese Buddhism. And it conformed. Here's where it can get very interesting, and in China did. Similarly, as Zen came to Japan, it was essential to its acceptance that it found a useful place within society.

And, we're at an interesting moment in the West when our religions are loosening their hold on us. It's less important that the state, that the formal institutions of our culture, accept it. Decline and chaos open some very interesting doors.

Right now, we can open ourselves in ways that invite us to reengage our traditions.

I've seen three principally. One is doubling down the embracing of fundamentalisms of various stripes. The other is picking and choosing among the bones for useful bits. Often the word "secular" is attached to these attempts at salvaging practices. In Zen, for example, meditation is tied to brain waves. And success is measured by stress reduction. But there is a third way. That way of rejecting literalisms of various sorts, but seeing that the tradition invites us to explore the nature of the heart and the healing of the great hurt of our human condition.

A while back BBC produced a wonderful six-part history of Christianity written and presented by the scholar, Diarmaid MacCulloch. I recommend it. In the first episode, Professor MacCulloch talked briefly about the Oriental Orthodox churches. These are ancient churches that do not belong to the Eastern Orthodox communion, which is held together by their relationship with the Patriarch of Constantinople.

In that first episode, he interviewed a professor from a seminary of the Syriac Orthodox Church. The professor opined that part of why things went so terribly wrong in the Latin church, by which he meant the Roman church and all the Protestant churches that broke away from it was that their theologians were all philosophers. As opposed, he offered, to his church, where theologians were all poets and icon painters, artists of the heart.

I was so taken with that.

We are always in danger of being philosophers, when what we need are poets and artists. There's a place for the philosophy of things. A very important place. But as we engage the matter of life and death, as we take up the Zen way, we're being invited into the place of poetry.

Awakening is always like finding a poem. It touches and transforms.

We want things made concrete, once and for all. When, as it turns out, everything is wildly dynamic, composed of many instances coming together for an instant. And then reconfiguring in new ways. It is nearly impossible to capture such a thing in prose. Although we can get close. And, as the professor noted, poets and artists get even closer to the reality of things.

My old Zen teacher John Tarrant has been part of the attempt to bring poetry and art into our contemporary Zen lives. He invites us to reclaim old words from the West like spirit and soul and to find how they exist as living perspectives of a whole life.

We have a terrible tendency to divide our lives between what we can touch and measure and what lives wild in our dreams. That gap is a terrible wound. Here I return to those phrases, "form is emptiness, and emptiness is form," and "you are not it, but in truth it is you."

As we live into our Zen lives, as we take up the practices and open ourselves to the mysterious unity of the many parts, things happen. We encounter disruptions of time and space, disruptions of our perceptions of reality. And with those disruptions we discover openings for us into new ways of being.

It's a call into what I think of as magical realism. Or, if magical realism doesn't work for you, perhaps like the Norwegian novelist and Nobel laureate, Jon Fosse, call this mystical realism.

The French poet Paul Éluard, as translated by the Canadian Zen poet Peter Levitt, tells us, "There is another world, and it is this one." That. This. Here in that world, in this world of dream and icon painting, here we find the spiritual within religions.

For me, this is the great gift. What some call an "enchanted secular," and others the "magical real." Good terms. Such literary and artistic styles seem to come mighty close to what so many people have found on this mysterious path of life and intimacy. It is the heart, as I've found it, of Zen's gift.

It is the awakened view.

As a literary phenomenon, magical realism presents the world as clearly and accurately as possible. Realistically. But then there are left turns. Magical elements. The odd confusion between fantasy and reality. Hints of the supernatural, echoes of ancient magic. Just like with Zen.

Zen is mystical realism. Its magical realism is finding a larger view of the world. Yet, it realizes what we see and what we think are the tips of several icebergs. It doesn't ignore the material. It embraces it with abandon. In each breath. With each touch. And there is a deep in that touch. A dazzling darkness in that seeing.

Zen, taken respectfully, taken with abandon and love, taken fully. Zen lived intimately is a way of magical realism. The truth of the poem.

If we want to touch reality, we need to allow reality to be. For human beings, it presents as a wonderful pageant, a tapestry, an icon. A poem. If we allow ourselves to be guided by religion as poetry, as something subtle and dynamic, as something to be experienced, then wonders await.

What is awakening? It is opening our senses, resting in the mystery, and finding the magical real.

ZEN IN A NEW WORLD

> *"As I feel the grief of loss, I also celebrate this interdependent life in which we hold each other up, and mutually create the world. This world is empty of permanent, unchangeable things, and full of mutable, vibrant, complex, relational life. A life in which, when we can allow ourselves to feel each other's pain, we heal each other's pain."*
> (Susan Zesho O'Connell)[1]

Zen entered North American consciousness first through artistic and literary circles. By the time that crowd noticed the immigrant communities who had been there well before the handful of Beat poets and academics took notice, Zen was firmly entrenched for the majority as a counter-cultural phenomenon.

There continues to be a strong cultural reinforcing component to immigrant Buddhist communities, including Japanese Zen, Korean Zen, and Chinese pan-Mahayana which includes Zen. While significant parts of these communities are about preserving aspects of cultural heritage, this is gradually becoming more attenuated than in the original culture. It becomes part of a sense of hyphenation, a thing, and an important thing. But also held more loosely. And among those communities not significantly connected to Asian roots, the breakdown of that aspect of

---

[1] Rev. Zesho Susan O'Connell, "Intimacy with Suffering," Huffington Post, revised February 11, 2013, https://www.huffpost.com/entry/intimacy-with-suffering-feel-the-pain-heal-the-pain_b_2325731.

religion devoted to cultural definition, cohesion, and transmission is nearly complete.

This noted, there remains a tragic divide between so-called convert and birthright Zen communities. It's a recapitulation of Dr. Martin Luther King's bitter observation of how Sunday morning presents the most segregated hour of the week. Zen temples and centers tend to have a dominant ethnic culture and everyone else struggles to find a place. Bridging this divide feels an important project, maybe a critical project, as Zen takes root here in the West.

Whether there will be a reformation with greater emphasis on the cultural aspects of religion in North American and western Zen sanghas, is impossible to know with certainty. But, given the fragmentation of religious ties to cultural definition writ large, it's hard to see what any reformation might look like.

From that I would say the imaginal West offers several gifts and some challenges to our emerging Western Zens. Zens in the plural.

The first of these unique gifts of Zen in the West is the "Zen center." Mentioned earlier, the term itself was coined by students of the late Shunryu Suzuki. It represents a major shift in the locus of practice from monastery to lay practitioners. There are and always have been lay Zen practitioners. But they've been at the edges of the monastic focus. Here, that is no longer the case. The majority of people who practice Zen are laypeople and their communities are structured as Zen centers.

The second is gender equality, and with it, an egalitarian bias. In East Asia, there have always been women practitioners, but they have been marginalized. Too often even the literature reduces them to unnamed "tea ladies." The aspiring teacher meets her. Then after being bested by her, asks where he, always a he, might find a suitable teacher. She, almost always a she, then points them on.

Today, women and men seem to practice in near equal numbers. When surveying the names of the more prominent women teachers, it looks like there is solid parity. Not a done deal, not by a long shot, but the quest for gender equity in practice in western Zen is more than aspirational. Similarly, sexual minorities have found a place within Zen practice that is unusual among larger religious communities. Again, we are at a better than aspirational stage.

We have arrived at a moment where the first Zen priests and teachers of African descent are emerging. But whether Zen will continue to be practiced primarily by the white middle class is a real question. In a culture driving relentlessly in a multi-racial, multi-cultural direction with strong pushback all along the way—well, I already said, it's messy.

Now, the unique characteristics of Zen come West are rather more than those I hold up as great gifts. In addition to vastly greater gender inclusivity, and an emphasis on lay and non-monastic practice, there are two other facts on the ground. Whether they're gifts or challenges, they're with us. First is a de-emphasizing of ritual and other traditional temple aspects of religious life. Perhaps this is related to a lack of substantial overarching denominational structures. And, second, there is a deemphasizing of merit. In many cultures, for centuries, the creation and transference of merit was central to practice.[2]

These may be gifts, but they definitely are problems as well. Here we find that term "container." And here we find a challenge.

In East Asia, Zen Buddhism arrived in a new culture seeking support from authoritarian leaders who had the ability to either support or suppress. It was critical for Zen missionaries to be seen as useful to the state in some manner. Often this turned on the dedication of merit to benefit the leaders as well as the general

---

[2] Thanks to Stephen Slottow, personal correspondence.

well-being of the community. These aspects of religion as holders of culture are historically critical to the success of a religion. Another wrinkle on the complex relationships of religion as an aspect of culture. But there's a bottom line in this. Don't rock the boat. Do not annoy the king.

Then. Now. Here, Zen encountered bourgeois republics with declining interest in religion. Here, new problems emerge. And there is one thing we can be sure of in this: Issues of gender, class, and one definition of race or another, are never far from human relationships. Blend in how we meet our larger social structures, and it's messy.

The way we are organized makes our communities largely pay-as-you-go. The pressures to support the emerging sanghas and their teachers can complicate the relationship between teachers and students. As a result, it is hard to be poor, or even just struggling financially and be a serious Zen practitioner—in the sense of participating regularly and especially attending retreats.

I believe the very survival of the tradition may be bound up with how open the Zen centers really are. And, more. I've saved the biggest of the questions for last. With the challenges clustered around questions of whether Zen is spiritual or religious it's all pretty wide open. It is sometimes hard to see the container. However, something is emerging. Whether it's old or new is a question, but something is happening.

What we see in the rising Zen movement in the global north is a growing universalistic perspective. That larger one, which sees connections across boundaries, and some essential commonality. It is helped along by the subtle shifts out of the ongoing, sometimes unconscious, dialogue with the secular and scientific perspectives of the educated classes which continues to be the principal source of new Zen practitioners.

Instead of identifying completely with a nation, we are finding another and larger sense of identity. The themes of this universalism are all about interdependence. When we've turned away from the idea of our religion as a safeguard to some culture, and the work of religion is not seen as specifically guarding our culture, telling us who is in and who is out, then we begin to see something else.

It tells us of a small shift: A turning of the heart. A realization, an awakening. The new vision. Really, it's as ancient as human hearts, but stated unequivocally, is that everything is holy. Larded through all of existence. For me it is related to that animist insight, the world is full of persons, only some of whom are people. It is a song of the good and the ill, in the heaven experiences, and in those hell realms. It sings of some holiness that unites everything.

Another wonderful word arising out of our experiencing of a magical, a mystical real. And that is holy.

Our English word *holy* comes from Old English and is related to a German word. It means blessed. Holy is also connected with whole. It hints at our seeing the connections. It is about what we experience when we find those connections beyond the parochial. It doesn't deny the parochial, the intimate, but it does call us to something larger.

In practical terms it means contemporary Zen Buddhist political engagement is largely informed by something that no one culture can claim as its own. There is nothing that can be excluded from it. To see the other in oneself is to find a form of love. In a final and in a terrible sense, what love tells us, is that there is no other to be excluded.

Not precisely one. Not exactly two. But rather a dynamic intimacy. Love, lover, and beloved, are all facets of the divine. In love everything is holy.

It makes for messy politics. One obvious example: It challenges any idea of a border. It doesn't say they don't exist. It doesn't say they shouldn't exist. But it does say they're permeable in ways that challenge all ideas of ultimate separation. And, more. It calls us into caring deeply and doing what we can for those on both sides of any border.

With that, all things, intimate. As they are, you and me. The only difference, is, well, a new perspective. A wild and open thing. Songs of intimacy. Songs of love. In an era of fear, compounded by those who want to direct the fear at others, all of a sudden, our faith tradition throws our lot in with those others.

And it doesn't have to be this way. There is a strong counter current within American Zen communities. People who feel the progressive spirit has gone too far. The recent national American election reveals a long simmering rift within our culture. Whether this represents a rejection of liberalism is not yet certain.

Today most Zen communities in the West are socially liberal. If this continues, Zen in the West will be joining the other religious communities who share this new, universalist perspective. And perhaps in this new age, this crossing of boundaries will be the politics of Zen Buddhism in the West.

CONCLUSION

THE OX'S TAIL

> "It is like an Ox that passes through a latticed window. Its head, its horns, and its four legs all pass through. So, why can't its tail also pass through?"
> (Gateless Gate)[1]

The editor of the Gateless Gate, that most wonderful early thirteenth century spiritual compendium of Zen's wisdom, Wumen Huikai, throws in the briefest of sermons reflecting on the case. My profession for a quarter century has been preaching sermons. There are few I've spoken or heard as useful to healing the hurt of human hearts as this one.

"If you can get upside down with this one, discern it clearly, and give a turning word to it, then you can meet the Four Obligations above and give comfort to the Three Existences below. But if it is not yet clear, pay close attention to this tail and you will resolve it at last."

Our four obligations are to our family, to our community, to all beings, and to the great way. The three existences are past, present, and future. So, finding the upside down and penetrating to its deepest core heals the whole world right to the depths of deepest time. Then, together with that assertion, we are invited to pay attention to the tail in this metaphor of an ox escaping through a window.

---

[1] Gateless Gate, Case 38, author's version.

I've referenced that tail earlier. So, what is the Ox? And what about that tail? What is it pointing to? What is the invitation? As we come to the end of this book, introducing the intimate way, what are the crucial takeaways?

Perhaps the greatest of all koan masters, Hakuin Ekaku, ruminating in the eighteenth century, suggested this particular koan was one of the thorniest, one of the most difficult of them all. Now, from the inside of koan work, this isn't strictly true. To give an acceptable response for this case to a teacher of koan Zen is in fact pretty straightforward. To understand it down to the bottoms of our feet, all the way down, to let it penetrate through blood, bone and marrow; that is the hard part.

Part of why I'm a Zen Buddhist is that I see it as a manifestation of what is sometimes called nonduality. A term we get from the study of Indian religions, especially Hinduism and Buddhism. The nondual reminds us that we are individuals with actions that count, but that at the very same time we are united in some way.

For Buddhism, that unity is mostly found in an experience: not one, not two. I am not it, but in truth it is me. This insight doesn't ignore the ills of the world and the actions of people; it engages them. Our call to the work of justice is, to get all scriptural on you, rooted in a love that passes all understanding. To use an organic image, this sense comes from knowing we are one family.

So, what about now? Well, I see a great trap. What I see among the many good things, is that one deep flaw. It manifests as an undiluted optimism, and it is rooted in certainty.

Certainty is a very dangerous thing. When it becomes Zen, it is saying not only are we connected, but I know how. All sorts of ills follow that. I suggest our Zen universalism, our angle on the nondual, at its best leads us to a profound not-knowing.

> Dizang asked Fayan, "Where next?" Fayan replied, "I'm off on pilgrimage." So, Dizang

responded, "What do you see as a pilgrimage?" Fayan paused. "I don't know." Dizang responded, "Not knowing is most intimate."[2]

Zen brings us not to any kind of certainty, but to curiosity. It shows hesitancy in all things. It doesn't claim to have all the answers. It is open—wildly open.

Out of this perspective, I would like to offer ten suggestions. Ten rules of engagement inspired by the realization that, while I am not it, it very much is me.

Number one. We need to start with generosity of heart. We need to recall somewhere in the back of our hearts and minds that in some very real sense, we're all connected. And with that we need to assume good will as best as circumstances allow. It's not that if everyone gets all the facts, they will automatically do the right thing. But a more modest understanding: no one has access to all the facts. Not even me.

Number two. If we don't know, well, we don't know. And maybe it's best to find paths of harmony that guide us when we're not sure of what to do. Something external to our individual thoughts. I recommend something simple, something you find resonance with as a general principle. I particularly urge binding yourself to something like the Five Householder precepts described earlier.

Number three. We need to recall this is not all about ourselves, me. We count as individuals, you and me. Totally. Absolutely. Each of us precious. But never more or less than everyone else.

Number four. To find our way we need to commit to a relentless honesty, especially about our own thoughts and actions. We are not of use to ourselves or the world if we're lying to ourselves. So don't automatically believe everything you think.

---

[2] Book of Serenity, Case 20. Author's version.

Number five. We need to try for gentleness, aimed both at ourselves and others. Everybody is in a struggle. Remember that.

Number six. We need to recall we are never actually in charge, and it would behoove us to act in that truth.

Number seven. While anger can be the only appropriate response to some circumstances, don't hate. By hate, think of anger that never burns away, like napalm on the heart. It is hard to see the differences, but it can be spiritually fatal to miss this.

Number eight. A universalist Buddhism always seeks reconciliation, and as such ultimately is a path of nonviolence. How do we treat each other and the world if we're all family?

Number nine. And immediately connected to nonviolence, is to cultivate a sense of patience, even, even as there is urgency. There are injustices right now. And sometimes people are not in a position to wait. And all things come to fruition in their own time. Finding the harmonies and acting within the realities of our moment, is critical to any kind of success.

And number ten. This not knowing is a powerful and dangerous thing. We can embrace not knowing as a kind of soul-killing certainty. We do not know how our actions will turn out. Ever. There are simply too many moving parts. At the same time, we're not excused. We must act. And there are things to know, if provisionally. So, act as if you're not sure about what is best. Not knowing is curiosity.

Here's a truth. This Zen way is one continuous mistake. That's just how it is. I know how true this is of me. I don't have enough fingers or toes to count my mistakes, blunders, self-serving misstatements, and actions. Even fully engaged in the path of not knowing.

However, if our actions are informed by our intimate connections with each other and the world, and we find and engage broad guidance and something like these ten principles, there is hope. For us and the world. Taking it all up as aspects of the Zen path, I believe we have a lot better chance of doing good in this world than ill.

And with that, back to that koan about the Ox and its tail. It sings to us of our lives as they are. It allows us the vulnerability to not be trapped by our cultural assumptions, and invites us into a great mystery.

The question is put to us by the master Wuzu Fayan. I love him. He's one of those trickster figures about whom we never know quite enough, but he keeps popping up in our lives. Wuzu means "Fifth Ancestor," but he isn't the fifth ancestor, who is Huineng. This Wuzu lived through the last three quarters of the eleventh century, dying just at the beginning of the twelfth.

For me he is particularly interesting because the driving question, the heart koan of his life, came out of a conversation with a Sutra master, whom he asked about awakening. He was told "it is like drinking water and knowing for oneself whether it is warm or cold." Wanting to know that taste for himself, he launched into the great way. I've used that line over and over as the great invitation of the Zen way—to know for ourselves, for yourself, for myself, what is and what is not.

At least so far as the great matters of the heart are concerned, the great question that confronts us is knowing we are born and we shall die. After Wuzu resolved the question for himself he went on to teach. One of his students was Yuanwu, the editor of the Blue Cliff Record. A few generations later in his line we are given Wumen, the editor of the Gateless Gate.

Clearly, in this koan, we are given a metaphor, and the metaphor turns on the Ox and the Ox's tail. It's fair to suggest this Ox is the same Ox that appears that wondrous map of the way of awakening called the Ten Ox Herding Pictures.

In the Ox Herding Pictures the Ox represents our Buddha nature.

We encounter ourselves as we meet life and death and the most profound of mysteries: what is our source, our destiny, and our lives in between?

Buddha nature. So, what is this Buddha nature that is so intimate that it is like sipping that water, and knowing for ourselves whether it is warm or cool? First, there's what we know with our senses. Here is the flow of cause and effect, where we are woven out of many things. We ourselves, by our actions and intentions, add new strands to the great web. It is real. Pinch yourself, and you'll know it is so.

What about that tail?

Here we also come back to this quandary: the Buddha asserts there is no self, no essence, and at the same time tells stories of lifetime after lifetime, lives that certainly look like something with an essence. What I find in this is how that emptiness is experienced in our lived lives. Emptiness is fully in anything, as much as its particular characteristics. We experience emptiness as something.

On my way it has had three manifestations.

First, there was that separation. I feel it. I know I'm not you. And neither of us is the wall we face in meditation, against which our knowing pushes into not-knowing.

Then, through some miracle, a noticing. Realizing viscerally, deeply, truly, that I am connected to you. And you to me. And both of us to the wall. And, the Ox's tail wags at us.

The great emptying? But in what direction?

So. There it is.

The third manifestation. A great mystery. Our heart's revelations. A dance. A song.

The swish of an Ox's tail.

ACKNOWLEDGMENTS

When I was notified that my first book, published as *This Very Moment*, and a second edition, *In This Very Moment*, had gone out of print I felt a wave of emotions. The book had a long run. It was meant as an introduction to Zen; in the first edition it was aimed at the Unitarian Universalist world, in the second for a broader audience. As I reread it, I realized it was not the book I would write today. This book you hold in your hands is that book. The best I can offer at this moment in my life. But here in that place where I acknowledge my debts, I want to thank those at Skinner House who took a chance on my inaugural thoughts about what Zen is.

I want to express my gratitude to the good folk at Monkfish, especially Paul Cohen and Jon M. Sweeney, who saw something in my later take on the basics of the Zen way, and offered to publish it.

Of course, I need to acknowledge my Zen teachers of the formal sort, without whom there is no perspective from which to offer this book. Roshi Houn Jiyu Kennett and Roshi John Tarrant each offered me incalculable gifts. Endless bows. And then there are my less formal, but very real flesh and blood teachers, including Dr. Joanna Macy, Roshi Mel Sojun Weitsman, Roshi Robert Aitken, and Sensei Masao Abe. More bows. There are more teachers in this informal way, and that list is quite long. It includes practitioners and academics, and more than a few who think they're my students. I hold them in my heart, and I thank them endlessly.

I also need to thank friends who helped me think through parts or even read some or most of this manuscript and did their best to guide me away from folly. This include but are not limited to Sarah Bender, Omega Burkhardt, Florence Caplow, James Cordova, Phyllis Culham, Anita Feng, Michael Fieleke, Peter Gaffney, Claire Gesshin Greenwood, Chris Hoff, Kenneth Ireland, John Jeffrey, Richard Kollmar, Janine Larsen, Katherine Liu, Dana Lundquist, Rafe Martin, Ian White Maher, Edward Oberholtzer, Barbara O'Brien, Joshua Paszkiewicz, Grace Schierson, Stephen Slottow, Matthew Teshin Sweger, Tom Wardle, Mo Weinhart, and Victoria Weinstein.

And of course, my spouse Jan Seymour-Ford. Without you, none of this.